LUCID
LEADERSHIP

LUCID
LEADERSHIP

THE LEADERSHIP POWER OF CLARITY

Nicholas J. Webb
Chase P. Webb

LeaderLogic®
GOLEADERLOGIC.COM

Printed in the United States of America

ISBN 979-8-218-06685-7

First Printing

For general information, contact us at www.goleaderlogic.com.
To contact the author, visit www.nickwebb.com.

From Nicholas

To my amazing wife Michelle and our children:
Taylor, Madison, Chase, and Paige.

From Chase

To Nicholas Webb, my biggest inspiration throughout my professional
career and the best father a son could ask for. I would also like to dedicate
this book to my close friends and family for always supporting me.

Contents

Preface   ix

Introduction   xi

1   Reality Is a Valuable Commodity   1

2   Leader   11

3   Employees   39

4   Directors and Investors   69

5   Customers   83

6   Lucid Leader Attribute #1: Integrous   101

7   Lucid Leader Attribute #2: Mission Centered   113

8   Lucid Leader Attribute #3: Humanistic   125

9   Lucid Leader Attribute #4: Innovative   139

10   Expanding the Knowledge Horizon   149

11   How to Become a Lucid Leader in Four Steps   165

     Thank You!   177

     Acknowledgments from Nicholas   179

     Notes   181

     LeaderLogic® Services   185

     About the Authors   189

Preface

For nearly 40 years, I've had the incredible honor of serving some of the largest and most respected brands in the world. As the founder and CEO of a boutique management consulting firm, LeaderLogic, LLC, I work directly with the CEOs and boards of directors of my valued client organizations. Massive change comes at them from every direction: their customers, markets, emerging technologies, social change, workforce. They must master the overarching complexity of a modern enterprise. Working shoulder to shoulder, together we develop a keen understanding of their organizations and the challenges they face. From my point of view, my work allows me to acquire a unique and special insight into the lives of these amazing people and how they're trying to master the tsunami of market and enterprise disruption.

To write this book, Chase and I have leveraged over eight years of deep research and empirical experience partnering with dynamic organizations and solving their accelerating challenges. In all of our work, one common theme has emerged: Leaders are overwhelmed with information. The blizzard of data prevents them from seeing clearly. Because they cannot see clearly, they cannot make confident decisions.

Effective leaders want to be clear-eyed. They want to see through the fog of business. They want to arrive at simple, actionable solutions.

In short, they want to be *lucid*.

That's why we wrote *Lucid Leadership*. In these pages, we'll show you the incredible impact of the transition from disruptive to chaotic innovation, and why every organization needs to have a new enterprise strategy. This includes new ways in which you, as a Lucid Leader, innovate and deliver experiences for your customers, and the way you manage complexity across your market, your enterprise, and your own ability to improve self-awareness. You will also learn why the fastest-growing organizations have become masters at customer experience and employee happiness.

In writing this book with my son, we have made certain to include valuable insights as to how the new generation of employees see their leaders, careers, and work. We sincerely believe *Lucid Leadership* can become the indispensable playbook for the very brightest emerging and established leaders in the world as they continue to evolve their skills, insights, and future readiness.

NICHOLAS WEBB

As a young executive working as a business development leader in financial services, I'm amazed to see the corollary between Lucid Leadership and how it grows an organization. The senior leaders in the organizations with whom I work have leaned into a new philosophy that is human centered, contemporaneous, and thoughtful to the differences of the mindset of the new workforce. I believe that today's successful leaders have a heightened sense of clarity on what's really going on in their markets, their enterprise, and in their own sense of how they engage the new workforce to drive meaningful impact and scalable growth.

CHASE WEBB

Introduction

Lucid Leadership addresses an increasingly serious threat to the success of businesses from startups to well-established global enterprises. The root of this pernicious problem is the inability of leaders to *see clearly* and *respond appropriately*.

Too many leaders view themselves, their company, their employees, and their customers through lenses that distort or blur reality. They see only what they want to see, or what they hope to see, or what they fear to see. By absorbing information through a filter, and combining that filtered information with their own existing biases, and then making decisions based on this murky soup of assumptions, companies that should be robust and growing find themselves struggling. It's not because their people aren't talented or the need in the marketplace doesn't exist; it's because of a lack of clear thinking.

This book will show anyone how to become a Lucid Leader. Your organization could be large or small, new or legacy. You could be from any background. This book does not tell you which decisions to make for your company. It does not advocate any particular theory of business. Instead, we show you how to acquire vital information, consider your choices, and then make the best decision for your situation.

We begin by emphasizing that *reality is a valuable commodity*. This is especially true in today's rapidly accelerating culture of disruption. What was accepted as true yesterday may not be true today. The solutions that worked last year may not work this year. The Lucid Leader knows that the secret of success is—to paraphrase Alvin Toffler—the ability of all of us to learn, then unlearn, and then learn again.

To become a Lucid Leader, you must start with yourself. Unbiased self-knowledge is the foundation of clear thinking. It's not easy, because all of us carry protective biases that we think keep us safe. And lucidity, or the lack thereof, is highly subjective. As the book points out, there is no personal lucidity test! Why not? Because we live in a world where the consequences of a piece of information can vary according to the circumstances. A bit of data that seems unfavorable to one leader may be welcomed by another. The book uses the example of a shark spotted in the ocean. To a swimmer, this could be very bad news. To a marine biologist it might be a cause for celebration. Both observers would be lucid, and both would be "right."

How we respond to a given situation also depends upon our personality. In a business meeting, for example, each participant may leave the meeting with a different impression of its success. Some will think the boss is a dictator, while others will praise his decisive leadership. Who is "right" or "wrong"? That's not the point. The point is that the Lucid Leader needs to see this phenomenon clearly and accept it as reality.

Having learned to see himself or herself clearly, the Lucid Leader must learn to use the same approach with the organization's employees. We reveal how employees are behaving more like customers, and fall into various personality archetypes that have nothing to do with age, gender, or ethnicity. We tackle the question of employee surveys. Most of them don't work. They don't provide accurate information. This book offers a solution: the RealRatings system, which accounts for differences in personalities—and therefore expectations—as well as uncovering not only what employees *love* about the organization but what they *hate* about it.

Then we turn our attention to another powerful constituency—the organization's directors and investors. This is a special class of people with their own set of expectations, whose concerns are rarely addressed in typical business leadership books. But you, as the Lucid Leader, know that keeping your directors and investors happy is vital to your success, and the book shows you how.

And who could forget your customers, those wonderful people who buy your products and services. Their attitudes are evolving rapidly. They want more and expect more than ever before. They don't hesitate to criticize or praise your company or product on social media. Knowing what they love and hate about your brand gets easier with our RealRatings survey system for customers.

Next we provide a framework showing the four key attributes of a Lucid Leader: integrous, mission-centered, humanistic, and innovative. With our easy-to-follow roadmap, you can develop these important attributes and encourage your stakeholders to do the same. Lucid Leadership is a quality that everyone in your organization should have and deserves to have.

Expanding your knowledge horizon is a key element to Lucid Leadership, and we focus on artificial intelligence. It's coming, it's inescapable, and it's powerful. But some applications, such as worker productivity tracking, need to be approached with care. Lucid Leadership depends on a high level of *trust* among every stakeholder in your organization, and many of these tools erode trust. They must be used judiciously!

We conclude the book—we think you'll agree it's a fast read—with our four-step system for becoming a Lucid Leader. You need to get clear, become overqualified, embrace lifelong learning, and set up systems. Simple concepts, and if you take them one step at a time, you'll see the results!

Ready? Let's get started!

Reality Is a
Valuable Commodity

You're the CEO of a consumer products company. You sell on four continents. Your supply chain extends across borders to China, Mexico, and Europe. Your employees speak five languages. Your new product pipeline is robust. Your investors are happy.

Today, that is.

But what about tomorrow?

You're not so sure about tomorrow. It's complicated and hard to read. As you make your way forward, you feel like you're walking a high wire. On either side of you there's no net, but a yawning bottomless chasm. One slip and you're gone.

And now the wire itself is getting shaky. The wind is rising and storm clouds are gathering.

People all around you are shouting their advice. Some say that you should stand still. Don't rock the wire! Others want you to hurry forward.

Go, go! Some even say you should go back to some imagined earlier time when things were simpler.

In your own mind you're conflicted. Should you call for help? You've always been self-sufficient, and maybe calling for help will make you appear weak. But on the other hand, it's foolish to think you can do it alone. No person is an island. The greatest accomplishments are always done by a team.

But what about your team? Can you trust them? Is everyone equally dedicated to the mission, or are some flying solo, interested only in the paycheck? In your mind you review the executive group and top managers. You never know what people are really thinking. Just last week, one of your senior leaders abruptly informed you she was leaving for another company. You had no idea she was unhappy! But her move could not have been sudden. These transitions take time to plan.

Your customers seem to have minds of their own. Today they're buying your products, but tomorrow is much more uncertain. You do not have a crystal ball. Trends are hard to spot. You even hired a consultant to help you figure out a forward-looking strategy, but hundreds of thousands of dollars and weeks of meetings later, the future is no clearer than it ever was.

Your competitors don't seem to have much of a problem. What do they know that you don't know? Maybe they have better market intelligence. Or maybe just better luck.

But luck isn't a strategy. Luck is a gamble, and the odds are not good.

Your supply chain suddenly seems vulnerable. Covid-19, wars, climate change, political upheaval—all these things conspire to make your business precarious. The whole just-in-time inventory thing worked brilliantly when the world was stable and the rule of law prevailed. After that nasty business of the pirates working off the coast of Somalia calmed down, business proceeded without a serious glitch. But the smooth sailing didn't last long, and one day you woke up to the news that an enormous fleet of trans-Pacific container ships—including some carrying cargo desperately needed by your company—were loitering at anchor within sight of the clogged ports of Los Angeles and Long Beach.

Technology is changing at an unprecedented rate. More possibilities mean more complexity. More regulations, higher expectations, bigger risks. And yet you're the same person you've always been. You have the same brainpower you've always had. The same capabilities. The same values. These will never change, which may be either a good thing or a bad thing. Or more likely, a combination of both.

At least you're concerned about it, which is the first step toward finding the solution. Even for the most astute and focused leaders, the business climate today is challenging. Here are just a few of the reasons why the times we live in are so precarious—and also filled with so much promise.

The Rate of Change Is Increasing

Just twenty years ago, everyday life and business were very different. Depending on your industry, over the past two decades the products you sell have changed, or perhaps they didn't even exist back then. How you market them has changed. How you communicate with your market—your customers—has changed. The economic balance of nations in the world has changed, as have the expectations of your employees and customers.

Now think about any other period of twenty years in human history.

Has so much ever changed so quickly?

No.

Change—no, *massive disruption*—is accelerating. For example, you've heard about Moore's law. It's named after Gordon Moore, the cofounder of Fairchild Semiconductor and Intel, who in 1965 proposed that every year the number of components per integrated circuit would double and projected this rate of growth would continue for at least another decade. In 1975, looking ahead, he amended the forecast to doubling every two years. Since then, his astonishing prediction has held true.

Moore's law is imperative not just for people in the computer industry but because it's become a metaphor for the rate of change in industry and society as a whole. When you look around, you see that products are becoming obsolete more quickly and the level of service that was acceptable yesterday is no longer sufficient today.

Here's another example of how technology is progressing at an increasing rate. For tens of thousands of years, the secrets of human reproduction—specifically, why children resembled their parents—was shrouded in deepest mystery. For generation after generation, nobody knew the answer.

In 1869, a Swiss researcher named Friedrich Miescher isolated a new molecule he called nuclein, which we now call deoxyribonucleic acid, or DNA. From that point on, like a slowly accelerating train, scientists made increasingly rapid progress. In 1950, Erwin Chargaff discovered that DNA was responsible for heredity and that it varied between species. In 1953, James Watson and Francis Crick discovered the double-helix structure of DNA. But the idea of sequencing DNA—determining the nucleic acid sequence—seemed impossible until the early 1970s, when academic researchers used laborious methods based on two-dimensional chromatography. This led to the development of fluorescence-based sequencing methods with a DNA sequencer.

The Human Genome Project (HGP), an international scientific research project, was launched in 1990, and by April 14, 2003, had mapped 85 percent of the genome. A nearly complete genome was achieved in May 2021. Initially, the process was laborious and expensive, but costs came down as speed and accuracy went up.

In 1984, British geneticist Sir Alec Jeffreys began DNA testing for criminal investigations. The idea of commercial DNA testing seemed increasingly feasible, and research accelerated. Genetic ancestry tests were first marketed directly to consumers in 2000, for the purpose of reconstructing genealogies and investigating personal genetic heritage. In 2006, Linda Avey, Paul Cusenza, and Anne Wojcicki founded 23andMe to offer genetic testing and interpretation to the general public. By 2020, the company was worth $3.5 billion.

For countless millennia, we humans couldn't imagine or visualize DNA. We had no clue! Then, in just over a century—the blink of an eye on the human timeline—the floodgates opened, nature's secrets were revealed, and the DNA industry exploded in size and value. And it's only getting bigger.

If you look across the wide spectrum of human technology, you see the same acceleration. The breakneck speed of innovation makes it increasingly difficult for human leaders to keep up, and it's increasingly certain that what worked yesterday will not work tomorrow.

Leadership in the Age of Chaotic Innovation

You're familiar with the various periods or ages of technology that human history has experienced. They began with the Stone Age, progressed through the Bronze and Iron Ages, then entered the Classical and Middle Ages. Around the time America was first settled by Europeans, we were in the Renaissance, and then when the United States became an independent nation, we moved into the Industrial Age. This reached its height at the end of the twentieth century, when digital technology ushered in the Information Age.

Since the Stone Age, we know the rate of technological change has been accelerating, and much more rapidly in the twenty-first century. If we put the specific technologies aside—stone tools, iron weapons, industrial machinery, computers, etc.—we can divide technological progress into three periods of varying rate and disruption.

1. Symmetrical Innovation

For the first few thousand years the rate of acceleration was slow and predictable, and disruption was minimal. We call this symmetrical innovation, whereby innovations emerged gradually and spread across the globe incrementally.

For example, take railroads. The development of railroads became feasible because of two innovations.

The first was the idea of using rails to reduce friction of heavy, wheeled vehicles. Introduced in England in the sixteenth century, "wagonways" used wooden rails to guide cars laden with coal. The first North American "gravity road," as it was called, was erected in 1764 for military purposes at the Niagara portage in Lewiston, New York. Gravity roads—built to haul coal and timber—used stationary steam engines to winch the cars uphill, and they coasted downhill to their destination, usually a canal.

The second innovation was the steam locomotive. The first working locomotive was built by Richard Trevithick in Wales in 1804. Eight years later, John Blenkinsop and Matthew Murray built the twin cylinder "Salamanca," the first commercially successful steam locomotive, which was used by the Middleton Railway.

The combination of iron rails with steam locomotives provided the genesis of a transportation revolution. By the standards of today's chaotic innovation, the growth of the railroad industry was slow and methodical. In the United States, the American railroad industry began with the first passenger and freight line of the Baltimore and Ohio Railroad in 1827. The industry grew steadily, from 40 miles of track in the entire nation in 1830 to 8,571 in 1850, and then to 28,920 miles by 1860. By 1890, while the nation's rail network had grown to 163,562 miles, the technology—steam-powered locomotives pulling rolling cars—was basically the same. By 1902, track mileage was over 200,000 miles. In 1929, the nation's railroad system hit its all-time maximum of 429,054 miles. It has slowly declined ever since.

While the growth of the railroads was steady and massive, it was not disruptive. In other words, other industries did not suffer because of railroads. While the nation's small canal system and some river transport were impacted, railroads were an *added* industry, not a *replacement* industry. People did not lose their jobs because of the railroads. No factory owner ever said, "Damn that railroad for putting me out of business!"

We can see this across many symmetrical innovations. The printing press didn't make scribes disappear because there weren't that many scribes to begin with. Bigger sailing ships didn't put man-powered boats out of commission. The telegraph did not kill the U.S. Post Office. These innovations *increased* the market without replacing significant parts of it.

2. Disruptive Innovation

You might say that the era of disruptive innovation, in which one industry replaces another, began with Henry Ford and the Model T. The industry that he nearly single-handedly wiped out was the horse industry.

In the nineteenth century, the horse was the ubiquitous unit of power. In cities, they transported people via carriage and horse-drawn public transport. They were used for hauling freight and for farming. By 1915, there were estimated 26 million horses and mules in the United States. That made more than one for every five people. (Think about that for a moment—all the horse feed, the manure, urine, cost of boarding, space requirements.) In 1908, Henry Ford sold the very first Model T. By 1915, the company was making over 300,000 per year. In 1920, they sold over 900,000, and in 1923 the company hit its peak with over 2 million sold.

As the automobile ascended, the horse declined—along with all of its associated industries. By 1950, there were only 7.6 million horses and mules left in the United States, with 25 million cars and a population of 151.3 million humans. As producers of commercial value, horses were gone.

During the twentieth century, the rate and power of disruptive innovation accelerated. Passenger airlines decimated the passenger railroad industry. Radio, television, and movies wiped out the live vaudeville theatre industry. The rise of the suburbs emptied the cities of people. Petroleum products shrunk the coal industry. Vinyl records replaced shellac records, digital CDs replaced vinyl records, and then digital music files replaced CDs.

3. Chaotic Innovation

In our present era, we're experiencing disruptive innovation on steroids.

The rate and intensity of change are increasing. What was once a family-friendly roller-coaster ride at your local county fair has become a neck-snapping, gut-wrenching Super Killer Tornado at a sadistic theme park.

The primary effect of the Super Killer Tornado ride on leadership is that threats appear more suddenly than ever before, and they hit with greater force. In decades past, a leader could watch a new innovation emerge slowly, like a building wave, and—if he or she were motivated to act—take steps to mitigate the threat or even take advantage of it.

In the good old days, did many leaders fail to see threats as they grew slowly? Of course. The top brass at General Motors watched for over a decade while their business was hammered by Toyota and other imports. Their inaction led to bankruptcy—and luckily, a hard lesson learned, as GM has rebounded under new leadership.

Here's a statistic that shouldn't surprise you, but probably will. It's the number of new patents that have been granted every year for the past century. According to the U.S. Patent and Trademark Office (where they keep meticulous records), in 1901, the number of all new patents granted, both utility and design, was 27,288.

For the next 60 years, through the Second World War and well into the twentieth century, this number rose gradually, and in some years it even fell.

By 1961, the total number of all new patents granted—utility, design, and plant—was 50,964. This was a predictable rate of increase over previous decades.

Then the rapid acceleration began. By 1981, the number had risen to 71,064 for the year.

In 1991, it was 106,696.

2001 showed 183,970 in that year alone.

A decade later it was up to 247,713—more than double from 2001.

And in 2021, the total number of all new patents granted was 375,506, well ahead of pre-Covid levels. All across America, more and more inventors are churning out new ideas. We're also seeing a sharp increase in patent applications from foreign sources, most notably China.

Do *all* of these new patents change the landscape or pose a threat to an existing business? No—but many of them do. Let's say that *just one percent* of new patents prove to be truly disruptive.

That would mean that in 2021, the number of new and disruptive devices unleashed in the marketplace might be 3,755.

One of those new technologies might be aimed squarely at *your* business.

This is just one way that virtually every aspect of your organization is the subject of rapid and deep change. This onslaught requires a new range of systems, methods, processes, tools, policies, and even a new philosophy about the way in which you approach leading your teams and your enterprise.

Volatile Supply Chains

In the 1990s, manufacturers thought they had hit upon a brilliant idea: manufacture their products in the Pacific Rim—Vietnam, China, Indonesia—at a cost so low that they could ship them across roughly 6,000 miles of open ocean to the twin ports of Los Angeles and Long Beach, move them by rail and truck into the United States, and sell them at a lower price than if they made them at home.

This extended supply chain—in conjunction with just-in-time inventory control—worked well until the pandemic. Finished goods, parts, and raw materials freely circulated the globe. But by November 2021, a cascade of backlogs in the United States and abroad created a massive logjam. It started with a shortage of American trucks and drivers, while inland warehouses were stuffed to near capacity. Unable to unload quickly, container ships began to congregate offshore. As Bloomberg reported at the time, "Today's delays begin before ships even pull into a berth. What started a year ago with a half-dozen container ships that dropped anchor in the bay nearby has ballooned into a maritime parking lot that currently exceeds 70 vessels waiting an average of more than 18 days."

Ships that made the long voyage across the Pacific were forced to ride at anchor for another two to three weeks before being allowed to dock and discharge their payloads of thousands of containers.

None of this was helped by the lockdowns of major Chinese cities, including Shanghai, as the government attempted to meet its "zero Covid" policy.

Leaders are learning that buying components for your company from different countries thousands of miles apart can leave your supply chain vulnerable to both environmental hazards and political and social upheaval. Manufacturing of vital products in risky countries produces risk. A recent example we have seen is microchips, which are almost solely made in areas under threat of natural disasters like China, Japan, the Philippines, and California. And the war in Ukraine, which began in February 2022, created a massive disruption of oil sales from Russia as well as grain exports from Ukraine.

The bottom line is that disruption is all around you and increasing in scale and speed. You're not going to change that fact. But you can—and must—rise to meet the challenge. And the first and most important tool you need is Lucid Leadership.

Take Action!

✓ Looking across the wide spectrum of human technology, we see acceleration in the rates of innovation and disruption, putting us in a period of chaotic innovation. Identify the key areas of innovation and disruption in your marketplace. Are they impacting your business? Are you riding the wave or are you in danger of being swamped by it?

✓ The longer your supply chain, the more fragile it can be. Anticipate problems and be sure to review and recalibrate as necessary. Try to avoid long-term contracts with suppliers thousands of miles away in foreign countries—as the Covid-19 pandemic showed, you may have no control over these distant jurisdictions.

Leader

What do we mean by Lucid Leadership?

The key word is "lucid."

What does this mean?

"Lucid" comes from the Latin verb *lucere,* meaning "to shine," which is reflected in two of its meanings, "filled with light" or "shining." The adjective also describes someone who shows the ability to think clearly, especially in the intervals between periods of confusion or insanity, and whose mind is clear, or something with a clear meaning that's easy to understand.

In the sense of a business leader, to be lucid means to see without preconceptions, learn with an open mind, and act with transparency. The Lucid Leader perceives the world as it really is, not as he or she wishes it or imagines it to be. They make decisions based on unbiased, clear information, and if such information is not available, then they make the best possible choice among the ambiguous answers, knowing full well the risk involved. Life is risk, and no leader ever achieved success without daring to take a chance on an unproven solution. Such is the very nature of innovation.

Here's the Lucid Leader Manifesto:

The Lucid Leader

- Is honest about himself or herself.
- Sees the world as it is, without preconceptions.
- Pursues the mission of the organization.
- Strives to make a positive impact on the world.

If you're a Lucid Leader, you're able to:

1. Define the organizational mission. You see the big picture and how the organization fits into it.
2. Lead amazing teams that serve the organization's mission. You are completely clear on the positive impact you have on your team members, as well as the entire enterprise ecosystem of influence that includes partners, vendors, customers, and collaborators.
3. Meet the stated goals and objectives of the enterprise. You'll construct thoughtful measurements to constantly measure and monitor all aspects of your impact on the mission.
4. Deliver the reciprocal benefits of employee and stakeholder health, happiness, and growth.

It means being able to say, "This is where we are now, and this is where we want to go. Everything else is negotiable. Dear universe, show us how to get there."

For the opposite of Lucid Leadership, we use the term "fuzzy." This means befuddled thinking, poor planning, and lack of clear goals. A fuzzy leader is indecisive and too preoccupied with his or her own life and problems to set a clear agenda. Fuzzy thinking is vague and unclear, and fails to see threats as they loom over the horizon.

Your Personality

Every company is composed of four groups of people. They are:

1. Founders/Leaders
2. Investors
3. Directors
4. Employees

Ideally, every person in each of these groups will possess the attributes of a Lucid Leader. But because leadership brings with it significant responsibilities, it's vitally important that the members of the executive group—the CEO, president, and executive team—each possess the qualities of Lucid Leadership.

Where does Lucid Leadership begin?

Because you're reading this book, Lucid Leadership begins with *you*. Not some other person in some other office. You may be the CEO, an executive, or a manager—it doesn't matter. Your organization needs *you* to be a Lucid Leader.

This is not as easy as it may sound. Many people, especially leaders, will say, "Of course I'm lucid! I think clearly! I'm realistic. I'm highly educated and skilled at my job. I have years of experience. I will make the best decisions."

Here's the thing: being honest with yourself, and seeing the world as it really is and not as you would like it to be, has little to do with your education, skills, or experience. We all know leaders who are highly trained, claim membership in prominent boards and charities, hold advanced academic degrees, and boast decades of industry experience, and yet preside over corporations that lose money and fail to adapt to changing business conditions. On occasion, leaders of this type find themselves making the humiliating pilgrimage to Washington, D.C., to beg Congress for a bailout, or desperately casting about for a buyer to rescue them.

No, your ability to provide Lucid Leadership comes down to *your personality.*

The human personality manifests itself as individual differences in patterns of thinking, feeling, and behaving. It embraces moods, attitudes, and opinions, and is most clearly expressed in interactions with other people.

The word itself stems from the Latin word *persona*, which refers to a theatrical mask worn by performers in order to either project different roles or disguise their identities.

Where do our individual personalities come from? It's a complicated question, and the vast number of theories would fill this book and many others. Suffice to say we each have a personality composed of certain basic *traits.* A trait is a relatively stable characteristic that causes individuals to behave in certain predictable ways. It's the strength and intensity of those traits that account for personality differences. In a leader, his or her personality traits will cause them to see things in certain ways, make decisions in certain ways, and communicate in certain ways that will be unlike any other leader in a similar situation.

For our next step, let's propose five axioms that we can all accept.

1.   Every person has a unique personality. You have a unique personality. No one else sees the world as you do. No other person brings to the table what you bring. And that's a good thing! As Oscar Wilde said, "Be yourself. Everyone else is taken."

2.   No human being is perfect. You are not perfect. The greatest leaders have all had their attributes and flaws. With great leaders, sometimes it seems as though their attributes and flaws are both magnified to huge proportions! Therefore, the key to success is to leverage your attributes and minimize or somehow compensate for your flaws.

      The Japanese have a concept of *wabi-sabi.* It's the recognition of the imperfection of the world and its human inhabitants. It means that perfection can never be attained, and that instead we must strive for *excellence.* Good advice for the Lucid Leader!

3. In the human personality, the definition of "attribute" and "flaw" can vary according to the time and context. A personality factor that drives progress in one situation may be disagreeable in another situation. Today's perceived flaw may become tomorrow's positive asset.

4. Great leaders have had all sorts of personalities. Presidents Abraham Lincoln, Franklin D. Roosevelt, and Ronald Reagan were very different from one another, but their attributes blossomed in their particular historical situations. You, too, can be a great leader if you work with what you've got and put your mind to it.

5. In order to *work with* what you've got; you need to *know* what you've got. If you lack awareness of your own personality, and don't know your strengths and weaknesses, then you cannot effectively leverage your assets. You need to be as keen a manager of yourself as you are of other people.

As Aristotle said, "Knowing yourself is the beginning of all wisdom."

To facilitate the necessary process of getting to know ourselves, we first need to create broad personality categories. This will allow us to talk about human personality traits as they appear relative to one another. Then we can drill down and put your personality into sharper focus.

A Lucidity Test? Sorry, No!

I know what you're thinking: "Is there a test I can take that will show my level of lucidity? Is there some sort of scale with a lucidity score? Like from 1 to 10, where 1 represents total delusion and complete detachment from reality, and 10 represents perfect vision and cool objectivity?"

Sorry, there is no objective lucidity test. That's because while certain facts may be objectively correct or incorrect, like a balance sheet, the *significance* of those facts and what they *mean* to you and your company can vary based on your goals as a leader.

Let's say that such a lucidity test included a picture of a shark. (Personality tests often include pictures.) You knew it was a shark; that fact was not in dispute. Then you were asked what the shark *represented*. (Not its species, but what it meant to *you*.)

You might answer that the shark represented:

1. A dangerous predator to be avoided.
2. A beautiful marine animal that has survived on earth for over 350 million years. (This is true. Sharks survived the extinction of the dinosaurs 66 million years ago.)
3. A tasty entrée for dinner.
4. A really good character to star in a scary movie.
5. An endangered species deserving protection. (The oceanic whitetip, porbeagle, and smooth hammerhead sharks are classified as vulnerable, while scalloped and great hammerhead sharks are classified as endangered.)

Which answer is more lucid? That all depends on the context, which you can't evaluate in a test. For example, let's say the context is that you're swimming in the ocean and you see the tip of a fin circling you. Under such circumstances, answer #1 would be the most lucid. But if you were a chef at a four-star restaurant, you might choose answer #3, and be perfectly lucid.

Context can be very tricky!

For example, let's say you have an old factory and it burns down. You might conclude the destruction of your factory was a terrible disaster spelling the end of your company. Or, with equal lucidity, you might conclude it was a blessing in disguise, and you can now rebuild a better, more efficient factory.

You might look at the profit statements for a growing company and see that for the five years since its inception it has not declared a profit. Not one penny in any quarter. You might conclude that the company's business model was flawed and it should close or be sold.

This was the case with Amazon. Founded in 1995, in the fourth quarter of 2001 the company reported its very first profit of one cent per share, on revenues of more than $1 billion. This profit margin, though extremely modest, proved to skeptics that Amazon's unconventional business model could succeed.

Therefore—and this is super important—the Lucid Leader is able to see the world objectively and then apply that information to his or her own situation in a way that will help the organization reach its goals. To an outsider, the decisions made by the Lucid Leader may seem bold or even reckless, but to those on the inside those same decisions will seem rational and inevitable.

Leader Types = Customer Types

Human personalities can be found along a vast continuum of behaviors. Each one of us—leaders, employees, customers—has our own spot on that line. Because personalities are complex, sometimes we occupy a few spots, but most people have one spot that's dominant.

Because there are a lot of people in the world, as we look at the behavioral continuum we can group people into broad types. People are generally more introverted or extroverted, detail-oriented or big picture, leader-like or willing to follow, and so on.

Leaders are no different. They can also be grouped into types, and knowing your type can make it possible for you to know yourself better and become more lucid.

Let's get started. I'm sure you're familiar with *customer types*. That's where we'll begin.

Some readers will object: A customer? But that makes no sense. I'm no customer, I'm a *leader*.

Well, you are a customer in the sense that you want what you want. You have a certain comfort level with the world around you. You expect the world to treat you in a certain way. Your expectations will color your perceptions and your decisions.

Here's a quick little quiz to illustrate what I mean. Choose the answer that best describes you. We're not looking for perfection, just the closest match.

As a leader:

1. I know what I want, and I don't need endless discussions to verify it.
2. I need complete and detailed information about a situation before I make my decision.
3. It's important that the people around me—the stakeholders— believe that I'm acting in their best interest and they can trust me.
4. It's important that each and every stakeholder is on the same page and in agreement with the decision I make.

There's no right or wrong answer. Just choose the one you're most com- fortable with.

If you've made your choice, you've assigned yourself into one of the four recognized *customer types*. These also happen to be the four *leader types*. They are:

#1: The Driver

- **Assets.** You're a goal-oriented decision maker with a clear vision of what you want. You trust your instincts and your "gut." You may be capable of producing disruptive breakthroughs that defy conventional wisdom. It's likely that you invented or developed the core product or service of the business.

- **Liabilities.** You're likely to ignore or discount information that contradicts your vision. You don't want to hear bad news. You may resist changes to your plans, even if they are required by external threats. Drivers have guided many businesses to great success—but have also been gripping the helm when those same businesses crashed and burned.

#2: The Analytical

- **Assets.** You want detailed information, facts and figures, and you love to ask questions. You do your homework and pore over every possibility before making a decision. Much like a Driver, you don't value small talk. You like to stay on topic while discussing each option to ensure you're making the right decision. When you render a decision, you're confident you've covered every contingency.
- **Liabilities.** You may overanalyze and postpone a decision until you've seen every scrap of data—but by then it may be too late. You've heard of "analysis paralysis"—if you're not careful, this will happen to you! You may put too much faith in data even when it's flawed or misleading. You may value process over results. You "go by the book" and are suspicious of human intuition—but sometimes, intuition drives innovation.

#3: The Amiable

- **Assets.** The polar opposite of the Driver, you want to build personal relationships that drive the organization forward. To you, it's very important that everybody understands the appeal of the product or service. You may have a strong need to belong and relate to a group. Intensely loyal, you have a circle of professionals attached to every need in your life. You are dependable and you "go with the flow."

- **Liabilities.** You dislike conflict. You may shy away from tough decisions—such as firing someone—that you feel will make others dislike you personally. You may allow sub-par employees to slide by because you don't want to hurt them. You may underestimate the desire of a competitor to crush you and your company. You might make decisions based on whether they will make people like you, rather than what's best for the organization.

#4: The Collaborator

- **Assets.** You're skilled at building a strong consensus among people who may have differing viewpoints. Because Collaborators tend to be tactful and adaptable, you're often pleasant to work with. You understand the need to ensure that every member of the team has fully embraced the mission of the organization and will pull together in the same direction. You enjoy managing people and being the team leader.
- **Liabilities.** You may fall victim to the desire to ensure that every member of your team is fully on board before giving the green light. In reality, there are some people who will always be stand-offish and take perverse pride in their desire to zig when everyone else zags. Your goal cannot be to get everyone on the same page; sometimes you have to forge ahead. And sometimes a subordinate will nod their head and pretend to agree just because they know that's what you want, and then they'll either do nothing or even sabotage the effort. While working to build a consensus is important, at some point you may have to become a Driver and say, "It's my way or the highway!"

Personality Tests Are No Panacea

In the preceding discussion, I presented four simple leadership personality types, based on the four customer types. But human beings are exceedingly complex, and our personalities range across a wide continuum with a multitude of gradations. (In fact, it would not be inaccurate to say there are over seven billion gradations—one for each person living on earth!) For most people, having self-knowledge of your own type can be difficult, because self-examination is difficult. It's like looking at yourself in a mirror when someone is holding it an inch from your nose. The subject is just too close!

When trying to get a handle on their own personality, and their strengths and weaknesses, many people go outside of themselves and seek objective advice. You can go to a professional counselor, or you can take one of the many online personality tests. These services purport to compare your answers to everyone else's and tell you where you fit on a spectrum of personality types.

While these "one-size-fits-all tests" are seductive in their ubiquity and simplicity, they must be approached with a healthy dose of skepticism. The employee insights and psychological survey industry is massive, and therefore organizations will often automatically believe in the value of their services. But the Lucid Leader knows that getting accurate insights about any human being—including themselves!—and the things they believe and will act on cannot be gleaned through a survey or test. The only way to really understand either yourself or an employee is through a combination of multiple methods, which may include some surveys and some testing. And no matter how you approach it, you should keep in mind these insights found in my book *Happy Work*:

- Human archetypes, including those of you and your employees, do not follow any rules of age, gender, or level of education. Contrary to the endless psycho-babbling about "Gen X" versus "Boomers" versus "Millennials," you cannot generalize behavior on these superficial attributes. In any large company, you'll find employees and stakeholders who are distinguished not by age or race or how they dress, but by their individual loves and hates, which we call hatepoints and lovepoints.

- Every person enters, serves, and leaves the organization across a series of well-defined touchpoints. These touchpoints range from the first interview to career maturity, and ultimately separation or retirement. Their attitudes toward themselves and their work will evolve over time. If surveyed, the answers given by a person at the beginning of their career may be vastly different than the answers they provide later in their journey.

- Most employee rating systems are reluctant to ask the employee specifically about what they *don't* like, or they structure questions that elicit a neutral response. In order to get to an actionable employee experience rating—what I call the RealRatings system—you have to find out what your employee hates and balance that against what they love.

In other words, much of the information and opinions that you or any prospective or current employee will provide on a prefab personality or employee satisfaction test—they are two sides of the same coin—will depend on the *context*. Just like our question about the shark demonstrated, our research has shown that the responses people give can vary significantly as their position varies. If you give a prospective employee a standardized test, you may get one set of results, and then after you onboard that person and they've been on the job for a few months, you're likely to obtain a different personality picture.

Having said that, here are just a few popular tests that you can take yourself or give to your employees. And remember, keep your expectations realistic!

1. Myers-Briggs

The Myers–Briggs Type Indicator (MBTI), also called the 16 personalities test, is one of the most widely used free personality tests. The assessment groups the participants using four categories:

1. Introversion or Extraversion
2. Sensing or Intuition
3. Thinking or Feeling
4. Judging or Perceiving

The test results consist of a four-letter acronym that determines which trait prevails in each category, such as ISFP, meaning you show "Introversion-Sensing-Feeling-Perceiving." There are 16 possible combinations, with analyses and explanations of the drivers, habits, perspectives, and strengths and weaknesses of each.

2. Who Am I?

Using images, the test asks participants to select the most accurate or interesting photo tiles in each category. The quiz covers a wide array of topics and preferences. In total, the quiz measures and analyzes 15 personality traits such as self-control, conscientiousness, resilience, and sociability.

3. DiSC

This test breaks down the participant's personality into four main quadrants: dominance, influence, conscientiousness, and steadiness. DiSC quizzes present situations pertaining to social situations and asks respondents to rate whether or not the statement is accurate. Answers suggest the test taker's interpersonal style, which can help improve teamwork and relationships,

4. Emotional Intelligence Test

This short test evaluates users' levels of emotional intelligence (EQ), or the ability to identify and react to one's own emotions and the emotions of others. The test consists of 40 questions with two available responses. Once participants input their answers, the test scores them based on four quadrants, assigning a numerical value to each:

1. Self-Awareness
2. Self-Management
3. Social-Awareness
4. Relationship Management

5. Caliper Profile

Often used during employment screenings, this test measures how the personality traits of an applicant or employee correlate to their performance in their work role. When taking this test, the user answers questions in various formats, the most common of which presents a set of statements and asks them to choose which most aligns with their views. Other question formats include true or false, multiple-choice, and degree of agreement scale.

There are many more such tests. Some of them are little more than "clickbait," designed to get you involved in the website; so do some research before you start clicking.

Do You Project Your Own Personality onto Senior Hires?

Here's an example of how your personality can color the decisions you make.

As a leader, one of the most important things you will do is hire senior managers to work for you and the organization. Your company will rise or fall based on the people you hire and put into positions of responsibility, so you need to make the right choices.

In a typical economy, when you seek a candidate for a senior position, you'll find several who offer the necessary qualifications. They'll each have the skills and experience that would make them a good fit.

With the question of qualifications out of the way, you'll make your choice based upon "soft" qualifications: to be blunt, you'll choose the person you like better and whom you think will fit in with his or her colleagues at your company. While job skills can be improved or even taught, it's very difficult to change a person's behavior. You have to know whom you're hiring as a person, not just as an applicant.

In the next chapter we'll discuss hiring in more detail. Here we're going to explore how your own biases will color your perceptions of job candidates.

To begin with, let's get past any notion that as a Lucid Leader you would hire—or refuse to hire—on the basis of race, creed, or gender. You may have your own ideas about people of another race or about the opposite gender, but this is the twenty-first century, and no matter where you got your ideas, you need to understand that *lucid* leadership means *legal and moral* leadership, where you set the example for ethical behavior. If you have any negative feelings about people of a different color, remove those feelings from the workplace.

Having said that, let's say you're interviewing for the position of marketing director. You have four candidates. You've had them each take some tests, and the broad categories into which they fall are—you guessed it—a driver, analytical, amiable, and collaborator.

Because each personality type could, in theory, prove to be an effective marketing director, then the question of whom to hire comes down one question:

1. Who will be the better overall fit in the organization?
2. Whose personality will best complement my strengths and weaknesses, and those of the other team members?

While the question of the better fit in the organization could be decided objectively, the second question is highly subjective, and will be influenced by your view of yourself and your comfort zones.

If the driver candidate reminds you of your father, whom you revered, that may be a plus.

If the driver candidate reminds you of your father, who abused you and whom you want to forget, then that will be a negative. You're much more likely to hire someone like the amiable, whom you feel like you could work with in the trenches.

You're likely to surround yourself with people who are not threatening to you, and whom you think will do a good job for the company without rocking the boat. Who that person is will depend in a large part on who *you* are.

If you're a collaborator who always seeks to form a consensus, you may be attracted to another collaborator.

If you're a driver, you may feel comfortable with another driver, or you may take the opposite approach and work to ensure there aren't any other drivers—whom you see as potential rivals—in your space.

If you're an amiable, you may be uncomfortable with a driver.

Unless—and this is a big unless—you're a Lucid Leader and you're able to step back, put aside your own personal feelings and expectations, and objectively decide what type of personality will be the best fit for the position and for the organization. You have to be able to say, for example:

"The marketing division is sleepy and needs a fire lit under it. Joe, who is a strong leader and a driver, is the person we need to spur it into action. My own comfort with him is not relevant. As a leader, it's my job to get along with everybody and every type."

Or you might say:

"The marketing division is full of creative people who work at cross-purposes with each other. We need to get them on the same page. Mary, who is a strong collaborator, is just the person who can do that."

Neither of these decisions have anything to do with your personal biases—which is a good thing.

You may also consider how the candidate complements your own personality. As a Lucid Leader, you may say to yourself, "Getting out and schmoozing is not my strong suit. I'm the type who likes to stay in the office and focus on the internals of the company. Susan, the candidate for marketing director, is very social. She loves meeting people and being involved with the Rotary Club and the Chamber of Commerce. She'd be a good company ambassador. Because we have different personalities, I think we'd make a good team."

One Meeting, Four Opinions!

Having seen that your personality is unique to you and reflects how you interact with the world around you in much the same way as a customer responds in the marketplace, the next question is, how does your personality affect the way you exercise your leadership?

As an experiment, let's assume that we have four leaders in a room. Each has his or her own approach to interacting with the world. For the sake of simplicity, let's say that we have one of each type—driver, analytical, amiable, collaborator. We show the quartet a film of an executive meeting. It's just a typical weekly project update at ABC Company. We see the CEO at the table with his or her dozen managers.

In our film, the CEO of ABC Company calls the meeting to order. He or she welcomes the group and then reads a list of agenda items. These are the questions to be resolved. The CEO reviews each question and then supplies the answer. Such as, "Do we need to raise the R&D budget for the new widget project? After studying the data, it's clear that we should. I'll direct the CFO to transfer the funds. Are there any questions?"

The CEO looks around the table. The managers smile. "No, we're good," they nod.

And so the meeting continues until the CEO thanks everyone and they adjourn.

Then we ask each of our four leaders to comment on what they just saw. To give their opinion about the meeting. Here's what they say:

- **The Driver.** "It was a good meeting! Very efficient. The CEO showed strength and leadership. The team is clearly in alignment. I see great success ahead."
- **The Analytical.** "This was a terrible way to run a meeting. Where was the data? On what basis were these decisions made? Was the CEO briefed before the meeting, without the managers? The decision-making process is horribly opaque. This company will not last long."
- **The Amiable.** "It seemed good to me. Everyone around the table appeared to be pleased. No one raised any objections. They're clearly a group of people who like working together."
- **The Collaborator.** "What is this, a dictatorship? The CEO simply announces what he wants with no discussion, no input? Clearly the managers are too afraid and intimidated to say anything to contradict the CEO. This top-down leadership style doesn't work. I predict that within a year, half of those managers will have left the company. This company is headed for big problems."

You can see that having been given the *exact same information*—having watched the same movie—the four leaders responded to it in four different ways. They saw it and understood it through the lenses of their own personalities.

Now let's raise the stakes. We tell the four leaders in our test group that their company and ABC Company are contemplating a merger. We say, "Executive power will be shared. The CEO of ABC Company will become the CEO of the new company, and you—the leader of your company— will be the president. Based solely on what you've seen, would you endorse this merger?"

- **The Driver.** "Based solely on this film, yes! Looks like a good marriage!"
- **The Analytical.** "No! I cannot imagine working shoulder-to-shoulder with someone who makes decisions based on instinct alone and without a thorough examination of all the data."

- **The Amiable.** "Yes, I would. They seem like very nice people and we'd have a good synergy."
- **The Collaborator.** "No! I would never get along with such a vain blowhard. It would be a disaster."

We see the four leaders making a business decision that's heavily influenced by their own personalities and how they each perceive the world around them.

Your Risk Appetite

Every decision you make, from the innocuous to the consequential, contains a component of risk.

At one end of the spectrum, your decision about what brand of paper to buy for the office copier is not fraught with risk. But to be honest, as the CEO or high-level leader, you should not be making those everyday, low-risk decisions.

At the other end of the spectrum are decisions that may determine the life or death of the company. These may be made by you alone, or with the board of directors, or with your investors; but no matter how you do it, your own capacity for risk will play a major part.

Risk appetite can be defined as "the amount and type of risk that you and your organization are willing to take in order to meet your strategic objectives." Leaders have different risk appetites depending on their personalities. The other side of the coin is *risk tolerance*, which is defined as the amount of risk you can actually tolerate.

High Risk Appetite

You may be a leader like who enjoys the excitement of developing new products in cutting-edge technology, even though some of those ideas are likely to be costly failures. You know that the bigger the risk, the greater the reward, and you want the greatest reward.

In the workplace, a high-risk personality doesn't need the same level of verification or time to make a decision that a more cautious person would. High-risk personalities embrace new ideas more readily and are eager to act.

Characteristics of risk-takers at work include:

- They have a sense of adventure and want to try new things.
- They stay abreast, and even ahead, of innovation in their industry.
- After considering the most important criteria—not every detail—they make decisions quickly.
- When something isn't working, they quickly accept failure and move on.
- They may have an "ask forgiveness, not permission" mindset that leads them to act impulsively.

For example, in 2008, a pair of nearly destitute San Francisco roommates, Brian Chesky and Joe Gebbia, built a website to find lodging for conference attendees who were shut out of overbooked hotels. They found three people willing to pay $80 per night for an air mattress and breakfast. Sensing a potential market, they recruited a friend, Nathan Blecharczyk, to help house attendees of the 2008 Democratic National Convention in

Denver. The site, Airbedandbreakfast.com, officially launched on August 11, 2008. It drew hundreds of listings but didn't make any money.

Earning just $200 a week, the fledgling service was floundering. Desperate, the founders maxed out their credit cards and applied their design talents to limited-edition election-year cereal boxes —"Obama-O's" and "Cap'n McCain's"—which they managed to sell and earn $30,000.

Meanwhile, the trio noticed that their hosts were posting grainy, bleak photos of their listings. The team scraped together money to fly to New York City and visit 40 of their hosts, taking high-resolution photos and helping improve listings. Those better profiles doubled Airbnb revenue to $400 per week—the most growth they had seen in eight months.

Chesky, Gebbia, and Blecharczyk also spent time talking to those hosts. They realized that unlike guests of the big hotel chains who craved consistency, Airbnb guests wanted authentic experiences, often in funky or picturesque residential areas away from city centers. They liked bungalows and treehouses.

Willing to risk everything, the partners eventually snagged $20,000 from Y Combinator. In March 2009, with the name simplified to Airbnb, they attracted a $600,000 investment from Sequoia Capital. Other investments rolled in, and in 2016—eight years after its official debut—Airbnb became a profitable company.

In 2021, during the Covid-19 pandemic, the company posted revenues of $4.81 billion and net assets of $13.71 billion.

Low Risk Appetite

While the idea of effective corporate leadership and a need for low risk may seem contradictory, it can work very well.

Characteristics of low-risk leaders at work include:

- Emphasis on extensive market research.
- Incremental change and innovation.
- Fiscal caution—no big gambles that endanger investors' holdings.

- Organic growth as opposed to growth by merger or acquisition.
- Governance by consensus and collaboration.

In the annals of industry, perhaps no company typifies a successful low-risk approach more than Toyota Motor Corporation. Founded in 1937 and selling in the United States since 1958, Toyota saw the flashy, every-year-a-new-model approach of the Big Three American carmakers and went in the opposite direction. Perhaps because they could not hope to compete with the U.S. giants on that basis, Toyota focused on the continuous refinement of a fewer number of models. Nowhere was this more clearly shown than with the Toyota Corolla. First introduced in 1966, the company relentlessly focused on the Corolla as its flagship compact sedan. In 1974 it became the best-selling car in the world, and by 1997 had surpassed the Volkswagen Beetle for the most cars sold of a single nameplate. In 2021, the car reached a total of 50 million sold in 12 model generations. (The VW Beetle racked up 23 million sold in 81 years. The Ford Model T—the first car to be continuously improved—sold an astonishing 15 million cars from 1908 to 1927.)

The word for the Toyota approach is *kaizen*, which means "continuous improvement." The focus is on maximum quality, the elimination of waste, and improvements in efficiency, both in terms of equipment and work procedures. It does *not* mean radical change!

Another Toyota word is *nemawashi*, which means "laying the groundwork or foundation; building consensus." It's the sharing of information about decisions that will be made, in order to involve all stakeholders in the process. The successful application of *nemawashi* allows changes to be carried out with no surprises and no shocks to the system.

You might even say it's almost boring—if it weren't so incredibly successful.

What type of leader—what personality—do you think it takes to guide this risk-averse global conglomerate?

In 2009, Akio Toyoda was named president of Toyota Motor Corporation. Born May 3, 1956, he's the grandson of the founder of Toyota Motors, Kiichiro Toyoda. If you search the internet for personal information, you'll find nothing more than the perfunctory professional bio. Outwardly, he fits CNN's profile of a Toyota leader: "Toyota CEOs are traditionally gray-suited men who affect the public personalities of actuaries and personify the faceless anonymity of consensus management."[1] He's no Lee Iacocca or Elon Musk! But as the president, Akio Toyoda is definitely a "car guy." He's fully involved and hands-on, and a quiet champion of innovation. He's a qualified test driver and likes to race cars under the pseudonym "Morizo Kinoshita."

High risk or low risk: The only relevant question is, is the right personality in the right leadership position?

Change Your Personality?
Can a Zebra Change Its Stripes?

Once you have a clear idea of your personality and its strengths and weaknesses, then you may wonder about *changing* your personality in order to become a better leader.

This is very difficult. As the old saying goes, you might as well ask a zebra to change its stripes.

Your personality was forged in childhood through your interactions with your parents, siblings, and other family members. If you were the family peacemaker as a child, you'll be one as an adult. If you were a lone wolf as a child, you'll be one as an adult. If you rejected authority as a kid, you'll have the same attitude when you grow up. If you were told that you were too stupid to succeed (as I was, and I take comfort in the fact that the teachers of Thomas Edison told him the same thing), you may believe it—or you may spend your life determined to prove them wrong.

You may be able to cover these childhood impressions with the veneer of maturity, but they'll always be there, in your heart.

There's nothing wrong with any of this. Successful leaders and entrepreneurs come in all types. And it's not really a question of changing your personality as it is of improving your strengths. It's not unlike what a bodybuilder does when he or she focuses on one set of muscles to develop.

It's also a matter of being realistic. The smart leaders who prevail in an intensely competitive and fast-changing world recognize they view the world through a particular lens, and that others may see the same scene very differently.

Instead of thinking about how to become a different person, it's more useful to say, "I am who I am. I am imperfect, like everyone. How can I maximize my assets as a leader, minimize my shortcomings, and surround myself with people who will fill in the gaps?"

It's Complicated: Steve Jobs and His Personal Demons

In terms of their personal biographies, most corporate leaders are not remarkable. If you Google their early lives, you'll get the standard info about where they were born and where they went to college, and little else.

Steve Jobs is an exception. He spoke extensively about his early life, and much has been written about it. As a technology and marketing innovator, he was among the greatest, and about as lucid as you can get. But as a manager of people, he was deeply conflicted and difficult to work with.

Born in San Francisco, on 24 February 1955, his birth parents were a graduate student named Joanna Schieble and a Syrian teaching assistant named Abdulfattah Jandali. Not ready for a family, they put their baby up for adoption. Paul and Clara Jobs had been wanting a child for many years, so they adopted Joanne and Abdullah's son and named him Steven Paul Jobs.

As a child, Steve's home life in Mountain View, near Palo Alto, California, was positive and peaceful, but the knowledge that his birth parents had given him up was painful.

When he was about six years old, he confided in a little girl who lived across the street that he was adopted. "So, does that mean your real parents didn't want you?" she asked.

Steve ran home crying. His parents explained that with them, he always had a home. "We specifically picked you," they said.

"I've always felt special," Steve later said. "My parents made me feel special."

Even so, Steve constantly got into trouble at school for pulling pranks. He had a strong dislike for authority, hated being told what to do, and was suspended more than once.

In ninth grade, he took a science class. According to Mr. McCollum, the science teacher, Steve was usually "off in a corner doing something on his own and really didn't want to have much of anything to do with either me or the rest of the class."

Fast-forward to his leadership at Apple.

As early as 1987, the *New York Times* wrote, "By the early '80s, Mr. Jobs was widely hated at Apple. Senior management had to endure his temper tantrums. He created resentment among employees by turning some into stars and insulting others, often reducing them to tears. Mr. Jobs himself would frequently cry after fights with fellow executives."[2]

In her autobiography, *Small Fry*, his daughter Lisa Brennan-Jobs, paints him as someone who could be extraordinarily self-centered and mean. For years, Jobs denied being her father and didn't start paying child support until after a DNA test proved he was and a court ordered him to start paying. She and her mother lived in poverty, subsisting on welfare payments, her mother's low-paying jobs, and the charity of others.

If nothing else, Jobs was a man of deep contradictions. Walter Isaacson's best-selling biography offered a searing look at what the author has called "Bad Steve" and "Good Steve":

Bad Steve was spiteful, petulant, rude, and controlling; threw tantrums when he didn't get his way; enjoyed publicly humiliating employees before summarily firing them; grabbed credit for work he hadn't done; and even childishly parked his Mercedes in handicapped spots.

Good Steve was charismatic, brilliant, a relentless champion for excellence, and a business alchemist who turned a faltering computer company into a consumer products gold mine.

He was both incredibly blind about himself and incredibly lucid about the mission of his business.

Jobs biographer Sutton noted, "Even people who worked with Jobs told me that they'd seen him make people cry many times, but that 80 percent of the time he was right. It is troubling that there's this notion in our culture that if you're a winner, it's okay to be an asshole."[3]

This is why his legacy is so perilous: As Tom McNichol wrote, "Such subtleties may be lost on CEOs, middle managers and wannabe masters of the universe who are currently devouring the Steve Jobs biography and thinking to themselves: 'See! Steve Jobs was an asshole and he was one of the most successful businessmen on the planet. Maybe if I become an even bigger asshole, I'll be successful like Steve.'"[4]

And let's not forget that Apple cofounder Steve Wozniak said that some of the most creative people in Apple who worked on the Macintosh left the company and refused to ever work for Jobs again.[5]

Take Action!

✓ Remember the Lucid Leader Manifesto:

The Lucid Leader

- Is honest about himself or herself.
- Sees the world as it is, without preconceptions.
- Pursues the mission of the organization.
- Strives to make a positive impact on the world.

✓ As a Lucid Leader, you need to:

1. Define the organizational mission.
2. Lead amazing teams that serve organization's mission.

3. Meet the stated goals and objectives of the enterprise.
4. Deliver the reciprocal benefits of employee and stakeholder health, happiness, and growth.

✓ There is no one-size-fits-all standard of lucidity. Facts are facts, but their *significance* and what they mean to you and your company will vary based on your goals as a leader.

✓ The four basic types of leaders correlate with the four customer types. They are not linked to age or any other demographic but to expectations and attitudes. The four leader types are the Driver, the Analytical, the Amiable, and the Collaborator. Any type can be a Lucid Leader.

✓ Commercial personality tests are ubiquitous—they fill a basic human need for answers, *any* answers—but they are deeply unreliable. Approach them as you would any other form of entertainment, like Tarot cards or going to a palm reader.

✓ When hiring senior executives, base your decision on two factors: who would be the best fit in the organization, and who brings a set of skills that you yourself might lack.

✓ Know your personal and organizational risk appetite and risk tolerance. While there's no right or wrong here, you need to know how to make your organization succeed at the level of risk that you're comfortable with.

Employees

The previous chapter focused on Lucid Leadership as having its source within you, the leader. You are the center and wellspring for everything that follows, which is why it's so important that you know yourself. If you know yourself, you can ensure you're in the optimum environment for what you have to offer.

Look at it this way:

If you're an eagle, you need to be in the sky.

If you're a lion, you need to be on the land.

If you're a shark, you need to be in the water.

If there's a mismatch, you will not be effective.

This chapter will focus on your employees. If you think of Lucid Leadership as being three concentric circles, then you are at the center. You have the most control over yourself. Not complete control—that would be creepy and superhuman—but the *most* control.

The second circle is the lucid company. This is your organization—your stakeholders, employees, board members, investors, suppliers. As the leader, founder, or CEO, you have *some* control over this circle. Not as much control as you have over yourself, but enough control to make a difference.

The third and outermost circle is the marketplace. Here you have no direct control. The market is the Wild West of competitors, government regulators, computer hackers, landlords, social media, and your valued customers. It may also include your supply chain, especially if it's international. Because you cannot control the marketplace, you must be able to respond to disruption with speed and precision.

Because the success of any enterprise begins with its people, that's where we'll begin.

Like many entrepreneurs, you may be starting with just a handful of people, either partners or employees. Or you may be leading a large organization with hundreds or even thousands of employees and a significant board of directors. Regardless of the position you're hiring for—whether it's a C-suite executive or a front-line call center worker, the number one question that causes employer anxiety is this:

"Is it possible to know how a new employee will perform after they've been hired?"

This is key, isn't it? This book is about Lucid Leadership, and what could be more lucid than hiring a new person and, over time, seeing you've made the right choice. We've all heard—or experienced firsthand—horror stories of people who had perfect resumes and interviewed well, and were hired with high expectations, only to fail at the job. Such mistakes can be very costly.

This is not a chapter on how to hire people—you can buy a dozen good books on that important topic. The goal here is to provide key insights into how to make the process transparent and truthful, so that you can make a lucid decision.

Employees Are Behaving More Like Customers

Much has been written about the shift in employer-employee relations since the Golden Age of American manufacturing in the post-WWII era.

Just as employers are increasingly less loyal and look at downsizing as just another tool to reduce expenses, employees have taken the cue and do not take their continued employment for granted. To protect themselves, they're increasingly "playing offense" by keeping their eyes open for better opportunities—and taking them when they can. Just as you must pay attention to the prevailing moods and desires of your customers, you need to do the same with your employees.

For many employees, the Covid-19 pandemic was a turning point. Schedules were upended and offices closed. In some sectors, such as healthcare, employees were pushed to the limit and suffered burnout. In others, such as travel and leisure, they were given fewer hours or furloughed. People were quarantined at home and few were flying. Remote work blossomed, as did the use of videoconferencing.

Then came the Great Resignation. First identified in May 2021 by Anthony Klotz, a professor of management at University College London's School of Management, it put a name to the unusually high rate of employees voluntarily leaving their jobs. Causes included safety concerns of the pandemic, wage stagnation amid rising cost of living, long-lasting job dissatisfaction, and the desire to work for companies with better remote-working policies. High quit rates indicated workers' confidence in their ability to get better jobs, encouraged by a low unemployment rate and government financial support for many workers.

Oblivious employers were caught flat-footed. Employers with Lucid Leadership saw it coming, and quickly responded by adjusting pay and benefits to keep current employees on board as well as attract new hires. Researchers at the Society for Human Resource Management (SHRM) found that more than half of surveyed organizations (58 percent) reported that beyond normal yearly increases, they offered higher starting salaries and wages than the previous year.

Among HR professionals who said their organization had seen higher turnover in the previous six months, 28 percent introduced new or additional merit increases, 32 percent implemented new or additional employee referral bonuses, and 42 percent implemented new or additional remote-work or flexibility options to reduce turnover.

"Employees are leaving their jobs to pursue new opportunities in record numbers, making hiring and retaining talent a significant challenge for employers across the country," said Johnny C. Taylor, Jr., SHRM's president and chief executive officer. "It's a candidate's market, and organizations must respond by recognizing the need to think differently in how to recruit and retain talent, revisiting benefits and flexible work schedules, along with broadening the talent pool for open positions."[1]

Eliminate Preconceptions

Whether you're an entrepreneur looking for your first key employee or you onboard dozens of people every month, you need to keep an open mind about the demographics of a potential candidate. You need to focus only on a candidate's ability to perform the job and succeed within your organization. To underscore the importance of this, a suite of federal laws protects the rights of both applicants and employees. These laws include:

- **Title VII of the Civil Rights Act of 1964.** Protects employees and job applicants from employment discrimination based on race, color, religion, sex, and national origin. Title VII protection covers the full spectrum of employment decisions, including recruitment, selections, terminations, and other decisions concerning terms and conditions of employment.
- **Equal Pay Act of 1963.** The Equal Pay Act of 1963 protects men and women from sex-based wage discrimination in the payment of wages or benefits, who perform substantially equal work in the same establishment.
- **Age Discrimination in Employment Act of 1967.** The Age Discrimination in Employment Act (ADEA), as amended, protects persons 40 years of age or older from age-based employment discrimination. The Older Workers Benefit Protection Act amends several sections of the ADEA and establishes conditions for a waiver of ADEA protections.

- **Rehabilitation Act of 1973.** Sections 501 and 505 of the Rehabilitation Act, as amended, protects employees and job applicants from employment discrimination based on disability. This law covers qualified employees and job applicants with disabilities.
- **The Civil Rights Act of 1991.** The Civil Rights Act of 1991 amends several sections of Title VII to strengthen and improve federal civil rights laws and provide for the recovery of compensatory damages in federal sector cases of intentional employment discrimination.

A policy of inclusiveness is also smart business! The vast majority of businesses sell into the general marketplace, which is increasingly diverse, and—especially on social media and in marketing—you need to ensure your organization reflects your customer base.

Let the Applicant Show You Who They Are

Too many interviewers approach the task as if it were something distasteful or inconvenient, and to simplify matters for themselves, they scroll through the same boring interviewer questions: "In your previous job, what was your greatest challenge?" Or, "Name one thing you would improve about yourself." Blah, blah, blah. In return, they get stock, possibly memorized answers. The applicant aims to please and will happily say what they think you want to hear.

You called the applicant in for an interview because, on paper, they have the qualifications. This means you can set aside their resume. Instead, talk as if they *already had the job*. Treat them like a colleague. Without divulging company secrets, get the ideas flowing. See how they interact with you. For senior hires, you must ensure they have the opportunity to interact with the people with whom they'll be working.

Make Informed Hiring Decisions— and Never Need to Fire!

You know the popular saying, "Hire slow, fire fast."

To "hire slow" means take your time in hiring. Don't rush the process just because you're desperate to plug a warm body into a role. You need time to get to know someone and for them to get to know you and the job they'll be doing. You should only make a final hiring decision—and the person should only accept it—when both parties are comfortable.

But when you think about it, hiring *slow* doesn't precisely describe what you need to do. "Hire slow" describes the *period of time* you devote to interviewing and onboarding. That's a useful metric, but it's not the most important. In my work I've heard horror stories of top executives who have been hired slow—sometimes over a period of several months—and everything seemed ducky until suddenly it wasn't. In one case the performance of the new hire—a sales director—slowly declined until he was losing money for the company, and after a year on the job he admitted that the job was a terrible fit. After showing him the exit, it took the company another year to regain the precious ground it had lost.

In other situations, I've seen candidates arrive for their interview and be literally hired on the spot, with a happy ending for all parties. It can happen!

I've also seen examples—perhaps you have too—of people being hired even though there was no position for them! In such cases the leader thinks that the person is so interesting and brilliant that they want the person to join the team immediately, with the details to be sorted out later.

Have a System—but Be Prepared to Override It

What does this mean? As I advise my global clients, while every business depends upon the establishment and use of systems, at the end of the day, for tasks involving people, *there is no system*. Or rather, you can have a system (for hiring, for example), but blind obedience to the system can be fatal. You need to be able to say, "Wait a minute! We need to take a second look. We cannot allow a set of preconceptions to prevent us from seizing a powerful opportunity."

Here's the bottom line. For any new hire, you're going to have two questions:

1. Are the person's skills, education, and experience sufficient? This is easily determined from their resume and the interview. His or her readiness for the role can be quickly verified before an offer is made.

   If the answer is "yes," then you move on to the next question:
2. Will this person be happy working here?

This may seem like a weird question. Since when does being a happy employee mean anything?

Well, it may not have meant much 50 years ago, but it means a lot today. Research has shown conclusively that employees—at any level—who are engaged and enjoy their work are far more productive than those who are either resigned to their fate, bored, feel discriminated against, or are otherwise unfulfilled in their job.

The challenge is that many job applicants are proficient liars. That is to say, they need the job for a variety of reasons and they really don't care about anything beyond getting that first paycheck. So they'll say exactly what they think you want to hear. Then, after they're hired and the weeks drag on, the misery surfaces.

Many employers try to ask trick questions to elicit an unguarded response. For example, in the early days of SpaceX and Tesla, Elon Musk reportedly interviewed every job applicant who walked through the door. It didn't matter what position they were interviewing for—he talked to them all. According to his biography, Musk asked each of them his favorite brainteaser question: "You're standing on the surface of the earth. You walk one mile south, one mile west, and one mile north. You end up exactly where you started. Where are you?"

As most people know by now, the correct answer is, "The North Pole."

I would submit that the correct answer—or any answer—would not be a good gauge of the specific question of whether the person would be happy working for Mr. Musk.

So what might be a useful litmus test?

Here's one: How about the desire to engage in constructive conflict?

You Want Honest Conflict

Every business faces tough questions and challenges. Often—or perhaps usually—the solution is not clear. It lies somewhere within various competing solutions. Nowhere is this seen more vividly than when a new opportunity, such as a merger, appears on the horizon. In response, people often work hard to expand their personal turf while defending it against attack. Anyone who has a phobia of conflict and who recoils in horror at the start of a robust discussion should not be a part of your forward-thinking, aggressively growing organization.

People who avoid conflict are what I call "Extreme Amiables." This means they value tranquility and the appearance of collegiality so much that they would rather be a leaf in the wind than risk friction with a colleague. Such people might do what you tell them to do, but you don't want them in a position of leadership. *And they will not fight for the organization.*

The human soul is difficult to penetrate. People often do not know what they want and consequently cannot describe to you what they want. In my experience, the best way to determine if someone is a good fit for your organization is to ask them provocative, open-ended questions for which they cannot intuit a "correct" answer. Be blunt! For example, say, "The newest model widget that we put on the market is not selling as well as we had hoped. In fact, we're losing money. Some people want to terminate the project. Others think we need to invest more in it. What do you think? Kill it or keep it?"

Or, "We're forming a committee to discuss and determine the color we should paint the employee break room. Tell me honestly: Would you want to serve on that committee?"

The point is to get out of your comfort zone while you force the applicant to get out of theirs. Only then will you be able to predict with any accuracy whether your new employee will be happy to work shoulder-to-shoulder with you and your team.

Of course, for every Extreme Amiable who runs from conflict there's the bossy Extreme Driver who *seeks* conflict. These people are universally despised and (fortunately) much easier to spot. They are likely to be argumentative from Day 1, and you want them out of your organization ASAP.

With one exception (there's always an exception!): when you need to bring in a strong leader to save a sinking company from going down the drain. Steve Jobs is the classic example of the Extreme Driver. In 1985, he was kicked out of Apple because he was obstinate about what he wanted. He was a terrible team player and in constant conflict with CEO John Sculley and the other "adults" hired to run the company. Then in 1997, Jobs was summoned back precisely because he was obstinate and could reinvent the failing company. At MacWorld in Boston that same year, he introduced a new partnership with arch-rival Microsoft and made a statement that any CEO would be well advised to heed:

> If we want to move forward and see Apple healthy and prospering again, we have to let go of a few things here. We have to let go of this notion that for Apple to win, Microsoft has to lose. We have to embrace a notion that for Apple to win, Apple has to do a really good job. And if others are going to help us that's great, because we need all the help we can get, and if we screw up and we don't do a good job, it's not somebody else's fault, it's our fault. So I think that is a very important perspective. If we want Microsoft Office on the Mac, we better treat the company that puts it out with a little bit of gratitude; we'd like their software. So, the era of setting this up as a competition between Apple and Microsoft is over as far as I'm concerned. This is about getting Apple healthy. This is about Apple being able to make incredibly great contributions to the industry and to get healthy and prosper again.[2]

Replace "Yes-Men" with "Ideas People"

As leaders advance, they often grow increasingly isolated from the people they are overseeing. This may not be for selfish or egotistical reasons; as companies grow, leaders become too busy to personally interact with the growing number of employees in the organization. Over time, they begin to rely on a shrinking circle of close advisors. If those advisors are willing and able to articulate a variety of viewpoints and data, especially when those views and data conflict with their boss's thinking, this can be acceptable. But if the senior executives become a collection of "yes-men" (or women), they will cripple both the leader and the organization.

Yes-men are dangerous because the Lucid Leader depends upon a continuous flow of the unvarnished truth. The Lucid Leader must hear all the news, good and bad. He or she must hear all the options and weigh all the facts. Yes-men subvert this process and ensure the leader's decisions will be based on flawed reasoning.

The growth of the yes-man culture can happen for a variety of reasons.

- Because you elevated them, your subordinates may harbor feelings of gratitude and obligation toward you that distort their true thoughts, opinions, and how much they share.
- They may be vying with each other for your favor and believe that flattering you is the best way forward.
- They may be highly risk-averse and value their cushy salaries and golf club memberships, and reason that the best way to keep the gravy train rolling is to shut up and smile.

If you find yourself surrounded by yes-men who simply parrot back to you what you say to them, then to find the cause just go to the nearest mirror and look in it.

A culture of yes-men always comes from the leader, who knowingly or unintentionally communicates to subordinates that he or she only want good news and agreement.

It can be difficult to self-assess and identify this tendency because you'll be assessing yourself. If you've already created a culture of yes-men, it will be difficult for your team to change their mindset, stand up, and speak their minds. You may need to enlist a trusted peer outside your organization, or an external coach who can objectively monitor your meetings or interactions.

To avoid this deadly syndrome, in any meeting, never divulge your thinking until you have solicited opinions from your team. Ask the question and then shut up and listen. Let them offer ideas and discuss it among themselves. Turn those "yes-men" into "ideas people." And then, before you announce your decision, clearly thank everyone for their input. Be sure to stress that you're grateful for every idea and every viewpoint. Remember, you're going to go through this ritual many times with the same people, and you need to make clear you are not playing favorites.

Once you announce your decision, make it clear you expect 100 percent buy-in. No excuses! The decision and its effects or progress will be regularly monitored, and changes made as necessary.

Employee Surveys and How to Make Them Work for You

To get a clear and lucid idea of how your employees feel about their jobs, employee surveys are a necessary evil. Because you don't have the time to personally interview each employee to determine their level of happiness, you need to do the next best thing, which is to ask them in the form of a survey.

Before you commit your organization's hard-earned cash to an employee survey, keep in mind that you may find yourself in the clutches of the "survey industrial complex." These skillful operators develop a survey algorithm, convince an organization to have their employees complete the survey, charge a fat fee, and then report out to the client in a dashboard for their employees' level of job satisfaction. While this is a lucrative business model, it's of little practical help to the organizations that spend tens of millions of dollars attempting to glean insights that could be important to their survival. The employee survey industry is both massive and highly profitable: GlobeNewsWire projects the global online survey software market to grow at a compound annual growth rate (CAGR) of 13.04 percent from $4.870 billion in 2019 to $10.162 billion in 2025.[3]

In our practice, we've found that employee surveys need to be two things: they must be highly tailored to each employee and they need to directly ask the employee what they both *love* and *hate* about their current role. When the answers are combined, the result provides what we call the Net Employee Experience (NEX). While we believe this approach is superior to traditional methods, we also freely admit that no survey alone can give a business owner the information that they need to be able to drive a cultural transformation of happiness.

Unlike standard employee surveys, the NEX consists of three distinct stages. They are:

1. Pre-Survey "State of Play" Analysis

The Lucid Leader looks at the most important challenges and opportunities of their organization. A key question that must be asked is whether the organization is *ready* for change. If the people in the organization are resistant to new ideas—even ones that will measurably help them and make them happier—then the first task must be to change the culture and perhaps even provide training, so that leadership can then present them with new information they'll embrace.

2. Survey Design, Evaluation, and Reporting

Working with a professional, leadership designs a survey that embraces a comprehensive and thoughtful assessment of the organization's challenges, problems, opportunities, and needs. The survey results are evaluated based on the overarching assessment of the organization, which allows experts to create specific recommendations to target areas for additional inquiry. This is how leaders get the best insights and create an amazing results-focused happiness strategy.

3. Collaborative Ideation

The survey alone is not enough to get clarity. Special employee programs called *happiness hackathons* are highly effective at soliciting authentic and hard-hitting insights from employees. At these real-time events, employees are emboldened by other employees to honestly answer questions about what's not working and what really needs to happen in order to build a culture of happiness. In addition, individuals in group interviews can be leveraged in order to get useful insights that leadership can aggregate along with the survey data to build out specific recommendations on what needs to be done quickly to move the happiness needle within an organization.

Is this a more complex process than just sending out an online survey that's used by every other company? Yes, of course it is. But if you're going to go to the trouble of taking the pulse of the mood of your employees—which you should on an annual basis—then you owe it to your investors to do it right.

Remember that there's no one-size-fits-all employee survey. Different situations make different people happy. Some people hold a low-skills job and they stay with it year after year because they like it. Others strive for responsibility and positions of leadership and to be happy. You have to recognize and leverage these differences.

The RealRatings Employee Survey

The Lucid Leader wants employees who are happy in their chosen jobs, happy with the company, happy in their industry, and happy in the community and at home. This is not a touchy-feely concept, it's good business. Happy employees are more productive, more willing to take a risk, less likely to be absent, and more likely to post a positive company review on a site like Glassdoor.

The question then becomes, "What makes employees happy?"

It's a good question—and often very difficult to answer. Employees are individuals, each with his or her own aspirations and goals. One may just want the paycheck. Another may value the workplace camaraderie. Another might be working strictly for the health plan. One might be very sociable, while another may just want to quietly do her job and go home.

These are slippery questions, and if you focus only on trying to figure out what your employees like about your company, you may never get a clear picture.

In my practice, we turn the question around. We ask, "What do your employees *hate* about your company?" It's often much easier to determine what a group of people hate or dislike than what they like. For example, everyone hates being treated rudely. Everyone hates confusing or contradictory orders. Everyone hates bathrooms that aren't clean.

The Lucid Leader sets aside his or her preconceptions about their employees and dares to ask them, "What do you *hate* about working here?"

The leader is likely to get an earful! Most survey systems are afraid to ask these "hate questions," or they design questions that have a neutral response. Why? Because the people who administer the surveys don't want to hear about what employees or customers hate. It seems too volatile and too provocative.

This valuable "hate" information can be used to improve working conditions and the culture, not by trying to consciously make things better but by removing those things that employees dislike.

Either way—making conditions better or making conditions *less bad*—the net result is happier, more productive workforce.

The RealRatings survey asks the employee what he or she *loves* about their job and also what they *hate* about it. When you think about it, this shouldn't be so strange. People are quite comfortable broadcasting to the world what they hate about stores, restaurants, schools—and their own workplaces. Just take a look at the comments on Glassdoor.com and you'll see what I mean!

The RealRatings system creates a score of two sets of numbers: hatepoints and lovepoints.

- **Hatepoints** are measured across four negative experiences, from 1 (slight hate) to 4 (maximum hate).
- **Lovepoints** are measured across four positive experiences, from 1 (slight love) to 4 (maximum love).

The RealRating is the total of hate points subtracted from the love points.

The survey provides no middle fifth choice of "undecided" or "not sure." The offer of neutrality makes it easy for the employee to avoid answering the question by choosing the bland middle ground.

You determine the NEX by subtracting the hatepoints from the lovepoints to produce a score. This score is very useful because it's expressly asking what the employee loves and hates about the organization. This provides actionable insights that an organization can use to rapidly fix the dislikes to significantly improve their RealRatings NEX score.

How does this matter in real life?

It matters because if you want to improve employee happiness—and therefore engagement, productivity, loyalty, innovation, and all the other things that happiness produces—then it's just as important to *remove those things your employees hate* as it is to *strengthen those things your employees love*. Both are equally important.

For example, you might assume that offering free coffee in the break room is a benefit your employees love. After all, who doesn't like coffee? But you may not realize that your employees *hate* the fact that the break room is located at the opposite end of the floor from the bathrooms, and if they want to go to the bathroom on their break, they don't have time to run to the other end of the building to the break room. They don't care about free coffee as much as they care about never being able to visit the break room in the first place.

The Lucid Leader doesn't make assumptions. He or she looks at the big picture and makes an effort to collect real information from their employees. To get to an actionable employee experience rating, you have to find out what the employees hate and subtract that from what they love.

Yes, but Don't Employees Lie on Surveys?

When trying to figure out what employees really think and feel, we've touched upon a very important topic—namely, that many employees and managers are conditioned to tell the leader (or survey taker) *what they think he or she wants to hear*. Many employees, even on "anonymous" surveys (yeah, right!), will say to themselves, "There's no way I'm going to be critical of the boss! I'm not going to throw away my chance for a promotion!"

The solution is twofold:

1. The RealRatings system *requires* the respondent to say what they hate about the company, as well as what they love. Neutral or "no opinion" responses are not accepted.
2. The willingness of an employee to say something negative about the company is a direct reflection of the culture of the

organization, and the culture is under the control of the CEO. If the employee works in a culture of fear, then he or she will feel as though they have no choice but to speak falsehoods to authority. If the employee works in a culture of happiness and trust, then he or she will feel comfortable in offering constructive criticism.

The critically important fact that most employee surveys ignore, and cannot measure, is that *every employee has his or her personal set of loves and hates*. The Lucid Leader will accept the fact that some tension among many diverse employees is to be expected. The salespeople may have issues with the people in fulfillment or quality control, while the people in R&D may have criticisms of the people in marketing. A bit of healthy competition is good, as long as the company culture is one of respect, shared goals, and happiness.

The Nine Employee Emphasis Archetypes

Just like leaders have their archetypes, so do employees. In terms of the RealRatings system, there are nine "emphasis archetypes," so named because each highlights an *emphasis* on different aspects of their happiness at work. We're not talking purity or exclusivity, but emphasis or tendency. There are six positive emphasis archetypes and three negative ones. These emphasis archetypes include:

1. Leader

The leader archetype knows what they want and will make unilateral decisions quickly. They enjoy taking on responsibility and seek opportunities to manage subordinates. Remember to ditch the preconceptions: The leader archetype can be any age, any race, any gender identification, any nation of origin.

2. Dealer

This person places an emphasis on the deal they get from the company. The various elements of the deal include pay, benefits, career trajectory, and to a certain extent, job security. They tend to be a bit less loyal and can be swayed away from an existing job with a better deal offer. The dealer archetype can be any age, any race, any gender identification, any nation of origin.

3. Homemaker

This employee places an emphasis on the importance of their relationship with their boss and coworkers. They like to be treated like a trusted friend with a special place in the family dynamic. They are highly stable and are easily swayed away from an organization that treats them with love and respect. Homemakers may lack the drive and sense of urgency that's required from a leader and may be resistant to change. The homemaker archetype can be any age, any race, any gender identification, any nation of origin.

4. Analytical

This person needs to know every detail of the product or service. In a leadership role, the analytical may succumb to the aptly named "analysis paralysis," and postpone making a decision until they have more information. They can be highly averse to risk. The analytical can be any age, any race, any gender identification, any nation of origin.

5. Visionary

This employee can see and articulate a future condition, such as, "Every car ought to be electric." They embrace risk and often enjoy causing disruption. To be successful, they need to have great communications skills while being humble enough to surround themselves with talented people who can make their vision a reality. The visionary can be any age, any race, any gender identification, any nation of origin.

6. Performer

The performer connects their work to their own personal self-esteem and identity. They proudly wear the company logo on their ball cap and will tell anyone who will listen about the new products. They're terrific cheerleaders for the company—but may not be the best choice for making tough or unpopular decisions.

The performer archetype can be any age, any race, any gender identification, any nation of origin.

7. Quiet Quitter

The first of the three negative archetypes, this person has become more of a problem in the post-Covid-19 economy. The quiet quitter has been through the pandemic and was either unemployed or working remotely from home. Now they've been called back to the office, but their heart isn't in it. They may be physically present but their mind is at home, and they've made the decision to do the bare minimum necessary to get their paycheck.

Their lives have changed, and they place a high value on flexibility, putting more boundaries between work and their personal life, and shifting their mindset from "living to work" to "working to live."

Such employees are difficult to detect because they'll be very pleasant and agreeable to their boss. The RealRatings survey, which requires employees to indicate what they hate, can reveal them. The cure is to ensure that every employee *knows* the mission of the company and *believes in it.*

8. Victim

The victim archetype believes the organization is taking advantage of them and they cannot keep up, even with a reduced workload. They typically seek allies among their coworkers and will eagerly participate in office gossip. The victim may try to cheat the organization and are sometimes referred to as leech archetypes.

The victim archetype can be any age, any race, any gender identification, any nation of origin.

9. Destroyer

Destroyers live on a different ethical planet than other law-abiding citizens. Many are simply criminals driven by greed, and at the upper levels of a company, where they have power, they can do terrible damage. If you have the misfortune to hire one or form a partnership with one (Elizabeth Holmes, the biotechnology entrepreneur convicted of criminal fraud, comes to mind), get rid of them as soon as possible.

The RealRatings Survey in Action

Now that we've reviewed the underlying rationale for the RealRatings Survey, it's time to roll it out.

The goal is to ensure that every employee takes the survey that matches their employee emphasis archetype. If they don't take the survey that matches, then the whole thing is as pointless as a traditional survey. We don't want that!

It works like a calling tree for inbound phone calls. When a customer calls your main number, the first thing you do is ask them some questions to direct them to the person or information that will help them. The recording says, "If you are a new customer, press 1. If you need to return your purchase, press 2," and so forth. By being properly routed, they're matched with the service they need.

This is a form of "skip logic," a strategy that determines what set of questions the respondent is offered based on how they answered the first or current question. Also known as "conditional branching" or "branch logic," skip logic creates an individualized path through the survey that ensures the respondent sees questions that match their personality archetype. Skip logic saves time for both you and your respondents, and reduces the likelihood that the respondent will become bored by questions that don't matter to them, or provide a random answer just to be done with it.

With today's digital technology, it's easy to do this with your survey.

For this discussion, we'll use the six positive archetypes and the three negative ones. The negative ones—quiet quitter, victim, and destroyer—are troublesome because they are likely to lie. But we'll do our best.

Your employees will take their RealRatings survey online, either on the company's internet or through a secure portal. To assuage suspicions about employees being identified, set up a common computer terminal in the break room or an unused office and ask them to use that one. Hopefully your organization has a sufficient level of trust so that will not be necessary.

The first question will serve to direct or sort the employee into one of the nine archetypes. If necessary, a series of semi-redundant questions can be asked to make a more confident determination. The employee is *not aware* of the "behind the scenes" sorting. In other words, the survey does not say, "Congratulations, you are a leader," or "You are a homemaker," etc. The employee is blind to the inner workings of the survey, just as the company is blind to the identities of the survey takers.

The first question could be:

1. I feel that ABC Company . . .
   A. Moves quickly and decisively to get the job done for our customers.
   B. Is a friendly, congenial place to work, almost like a second home.

C. Values accuracy and appreciates my attention to detail.

D. Has a vision for innovation and moving into the future.

E. Pays me well to do my job. I'd be happy to work anywhere.

F. Gives me a sense of pride when I'm in the community.

G. Is the place where I go to earn a paycheck.

H. Is a difficult and demanding place to work. I often feel overwhelmed.

I. Is a money machine where it's every man for himself—and I intend to win.

Ask the employee to carefully consider all the choices and then pick *just one*. If you have more than one such qualifying question, you could ask them to rank the top three.

Based on their choice, or choices if more than one qualifying question is used, the respondent is then presented with one of nine different surveys.

While all surveys will have some common questions, each will contain some questions designed for that archetype. The survey presented to visionaries will be different from the survey presented to analyticals, homemakers, leaders, and victims. The survey presented to visionaries will include questions designed to measure to what extent the company scored lovepoints and/or hatepoints based on the specific expectations of visionaries. Likewise for the other archetypes; each will be presented with their own customized survey designed to measure how well the company met their expectations.

Here's a sample survey for the analytical. The employee is asked ten questions: five are designed to measure lovepoints, and five measure hatepoints. We *want* the employee to tell us something she hated. There are no neutral answers.

Survey for the Analytical

1. Using the scale of 1 (slight love), 2 (some love), 3 (love), or 4 (maximum love), please indicate your level of *happiness* with the following five job factors:
    A. The pace of work and your workload.
    B. The opportunity you have to use your analytical skills.
    C. The quality of project information you receive from your manager.
    D. The clarity of direction you receive.
    E. The tools and training you have to help you do your job.

2. Using the scale of 1 (slight hate), 2 (some hate), 3 (some love), or 4 (maximum hate), please indicate your level of *dissatisfaction* with the following five job factors:
    A. The level of cooperation among your team members.
    B. The product information to which you have access.
    C. How often you're asked for your ideas and input.
    D. How much your direct superior "has your back" and sees your point of view.
    E. The speed and accuracy of the reports you receive.

As you can see, the questions presented in the two parts are similar but not exactly the same. The reason we ask specifically for what the employee hates is to give the employee "permission" to express their true feelings. We're asking them what they don't like about their experience, and we want them to tell us.

Also note that many questions are particularly relevant to the values and expectations of an analytical. This employee is concerned with data accuracy and technical quality. They are less concerned with workplace camaraderie than the homemaker, and less concerned with being a brand ambassador than the performer.

Each archetype will have its own expected ratio of lovepoints to hate-points. For example, if the test taker is a leader, we should expect a relatively low level of "love." They are very pragmatic and tend to check their feelings at the door. With leaders, you want to eliminate hatepoints as much as possible, and then settle for a minimally positive set of lovepoints.

Survey for the Visionary

Now let's take a look at the same survey when presented to a visionary. Some of the questions are identical (functioning as a control set), while others are tailored for the homemaker's expectations:

1. Using the scale of 1 (slight love), 2 (some love), 3 (love), or 4 (maximum love), please indicate your level of *happiness* with the following five job factors:
   A. The pace of work and your workload.
   B. The opportunity you have to participate in long-range planning for your department.
   C. The support you receive from your colleagues and managers.
   D. The clarity of the organization's mission and vision.
   E. The tools and training you have to help you do your job.

2. Using the scale of 1 (slight hate), 2 (some hate), 3 (some love), or 4 (maximum hate), please indicate your level of *dissatisfaction* with the following five job factors:
   A. The level of cooperation among your team members.
   B. Your knowledge of the "big picture" and how your work fits into the company's future success.
   C. How often you're asked for your ideas and input.
   D. How well your direct superior sets goals and helps you achieve them.
   E. The speed and accuracy of the reports you receive.

With a visionary, you especially want to pay attention to the responses that relate to how well they understand and support the organization's mission and their role in achieving it, because that's what's important to them.

Again, these are just hypothetical, sample questions. The questions you ask need to be tailored specifically for your employees and business environment. A survey for a manufacturer will be very different from an internet marketing company or a retailer. The goal of the RealRatings survey is to provide you with highly specific, actionable information about what your employees love and hate *according to their individual expectations*. The slight redundancy of the love/hate questions will provide a verification of veracity (or not). For example, if a visionary expresses very low love for the clarity of the organization's mission and vision (question 1-D), then you should expect her to express a correspondingly high level of hate for her lack of knowledge of the "big picture" and how her work fits into the company's future success (question 2-B).

In this book, I've presented nine employee archetypes. This is just a sample. In practice, your business will create as many employee archetypes as you believe to be necessary. If it were relevant, you could add demographic qualifiers like age, but only if you're certain that a particular age group has its own expectations—for instance, if they want specific retirement packages. The trick is to quickly move them through the qualifying phase before they get bored and want to either abandon or shortcut the survey.

Before the digital age, producing this level of agility and granularity would have been impossible. The data would have been too much to process, and the "decision tree" feature, where the respondent is instantly characterized according to his or her archetype, didn't exist. Today, with our powerful databases and processing tools, it will be easy to construct a RealRatings survey system that presents to each respondent a survey that is concise and tailored precisely to their expectations.

The Current State of Work
(Mission, Growth, Deal)

It is said there are unemployed people and there are talented people, but there are no unemployed talented people. If you're a top organization, with Lucid Leadership, then many of these talented people will be taking their paycheck from you. But if your organization has fuzzy leadership—confused, aimless, poorly informed, even in denial about reality—then these talented people will be working for your competition. They will be reluctant to interview with you because of what they've read on Glassdoor and in the press, and because they may have heard "talk around town" that your company has poor leadership.

Attracting and keeping mission-critical talent requires that organizations focus on three key priorities.

1. **Build the company on a mission worthy of great talent.** This does not mean you need to lead a luxury brand like Cartier or Rolls-Royce. You could just as easily lead a company like Dave's Killer Bread, which as part of its mission pursues a policy of Second Chance Employment: hiring the best person for the job, regardless of criminal history. The company—cofounded by a convicted felon—believes that offering someone who is ready to change their life a Second Chance gives that person an opportunity not only to make a living, but to make a life.

   In contrast, a mission to "make more money" is not lucid, it's fuzzy. It lacks any specific plan for how to do that, or how to capture a market, or improve people's lives.

   People with great talent—call them Lucid Employees—want to work in an organization that makes a difference. It's about connecting your employees with your mission and allowing them to feel good about the work they do.

2. **Develop a robust and thoughtful personal growth plan for each employee.** An employee development program can help both new and seasoned colleagues to learn, grow, and advance.

   The need is clear. A survey by The Conference Board found only 33 percent of U.S. employees were satisfied with educational and job training programs where they worked. Among the 23 survey components, participants gave the lowest marks to the following five: workload, educational/job training programs, performance review process, bonus plan, and, in last place, promotion policy.[4]

In today's competitive job market, that can lead to higher turnover as employees show little loyalty to organizations that don't support them. A survey from Payscale showed that two out of three employees who quit their job named inadequate career development as a key reason.[5]

It's about your employee's ability to create direct linkage between their own human growth in their chosen career and job.

3. **Compensate fairly.** The number one cause of employee dissatisfaction is the wage package. According to the Society for Human Resource Management (SHRM), when determining job satisfaction, 63 percent of U.S. employees said that compensation and benefits are an important factor, second only to respectful treatment by managers. Compensation and benefits directly impact an employee's performance and motivation to work, and are important aspects of an employee's satisfaction at a workplace.[6]

Create a package in terms of pay, happiness, and work structure that is competitive in the current landscape of talent competition.

Having revealed the necessity of becoming a Lucid Leader in two realms—your own work as a leader and the internal functioning of your organization—and having provided sets of tools to accomplish both of those goals, it's now time to turn our sights to the external world comprising your marketplace, investors, regulators, and competitors.

Take Action!

✓ For bulk hiring tasks—like onboarding 50 new sales associates—you need a system. But when hiring top executives, aside from performing the required due diligence, *there is no system.* You must be prepared to think outside the box and go with someone who adds magic to the organization.

✓ Employees are behaving more like customers. You need to keep them happy—not with free bagels in the break room but with a culture of transparency, respect, and appreciation.

✓ Constructive conflict is a good thing! Executives who avoid conflict are what I call "Extreme Amiables." They are to be avoided.

✓ Equally problematic are the bossy "Extreme Drivers" who *seek* conflict. You do not want them anywhere near the executive suite—unless your sinking company needs a tough boss to rescue it!

✓ The Lucid Leader must have honest, factual advice. If your senior executives become a collection of "yes-men" (or women), they will cause you to make poor decisions and sink the company.

✓ To minimize the growth of the "yes" culture, in any meeting, never divulge your thinking until you have solicited opinions from your team. You want "ideas people." Make them tell you ideas that you know may not work. Thank them sincerely. Then announce your decision, which at that moment is final.

✓ To be of value, employee surveys must be highly tailored to each employee. When the answers are combined, the result provides what we call the Net Employee Experience (NEX).

✓ The most important bottom-line question is, "Are my employees happy?" To learn this, you need to ask them, "What do you *hate* about working here?" The RealRatings survey asks the employee what he or she *loves* about their job and also what they *hate* about it. The RealRating is the total of hate points subtracted from the love points.

✓ You determine the NEX by subtracting the hatepoints from the lovepoints to produce a score.

✓ You then need to reduce those things your employees hate and strengthen those things your employees love. Both are equally important.

✓ There are six positive employee emphasis archetypes (Leader, Dealer, Homemaker, Analytical, Visionary, Performer) and three negative ones (Quiet Quitter, Victim, Destroyer).

✓ Using "skip logic," the RealRatings survey creates an individualized path through the survey that ensures the respondent sees questions that match their personality archetype. Each archetype will have its own expected ratio of lovepoints to hatepoints.

✓ Attracting and keeping mission-critical talent requires that organizations focus on three key priorities.
1. Build the company on a mission worthy of great talent.
2. Develop a robust and thoughtful personal growth plan for each employee.
3. Compensate fairly.

4

Directors and Investors

In business we talk about "managing down," which means leading your subordinates at whatever level they are and you are. If you're a shift manager, you lead your immediate reports, which could be as few as a handful of people. If you're the CEO, you lead everyone who's lower on the organizational chart than you, which could include thousands of people.

We also talk about "managing up," which means taking control of your relationship with your superiors. Generally, it means giving your boss exactly what he or she expects. You need to understand what makes your boss tick (and what ticks them off) and know how to anticipate their needs. Sometimes friction is inevitable, but knowing the right way to bring a problem to your boss can help you navigate sticky situations. There will be times when you disagree with them, and that's fine, as long as you're careful to disagree in a respectful, productive way.

It means being the most effective subordinate you can be, creating value for your boss and your company.

As an executive leader of your organization, you may have multiple bosses—the members of your board of directors and your investors or owners. You might say that in dealing with these bosses, you need to be the Lucid Subordinate. You need to manage up by doing your best to create a culture of lucidity for everyone above you.

Your job may depend on your success at doing this.

The Corporate Pressure Cooker

While every relationship in an organization is a two-way street, it's exceptionally so when it's between the CEO and the investors and board members. The stakes can be very high, and both sides need to see and accept a common set of validated facts.

Given the enormous pressure that can be put on the CEO and top executives to produce a steady flow of good news, this is often difficult. In recent decades, the compensation and job evaluation of a CEO have become increasingly tied to the stock price. When the stock price goes up, the CEO is a hero. When the stock price slumps, regardless of the reasons, the CEO is a loser. Job performance is also tied to quarterly earnings reports. Investors of the non–Warren Buffett variety are increasingly impatient and view a quarterly loss, for whatever reason, as a failure.

This book could be filled with lurid stories of scandals in which CEOs and top executives have lied to investors and board members about their company's profitability. But if you google the worst corporate financial scandal and the worst example of the failure of a board to provide Lucid Leadership oversight of an executive team, one name—which has become the stuff of legend—always appears.

Enron.

Like Benedict Arnold or Pearl Harbor, the name has become a part of popular lore. People may not know the details, but they know that something *bad* happened.

A Houston-based global energy company that grew at a phenomenal rate, between 1996 and 2000, Enron reported an increase in sales from $13.3 billion to $100.8 billion. In August 2000, Enron shares reached their all-time high of $90 dollars per share. Investors were delighted.

The company appeared to be brilliantly managed—but appearances were deceiving.

On December 2, 2001, Enron declared bankruptcy. The next day the company laid off four thousand workers. (An employee later revealed that Enron had paid $55 million in retention bonuses to top managers and executives just before going belly-up.)

What happened?

In an ethical company, the financial results reported by managers to investors are verified by the company's independent auditor. The auditor's work is overseen by the company's board of directors, which should be made up of objective, lucid people who have the best interests of investors at heart. This three-pronged system of management, auditors, and directors is designed to assure investors, who are putting their money at risk when they buy stock, that they are getting an accurate picture of the company's performance.

The chief architects of the scandal were the top executives: Kenneth Lay, Enron's CEO and chair; Jeffrey Skilling, head of Enron Finance Corp.; and Andrew Fastow, chief financial officer (CFO). When the company started to pile up debt and toxic assets, rather than fix the problem, Fastow orchestrated a scheme to use off-balance-sheet special purpose vehicles (SPVs), also known as special purposes entities (SPEs), to hide the growing cancer.

You may ask, isn't the outside auditor supposed to inspect the books and reject unethical practices?

Yes, it is. Enron's auditor was the accounting giant Arthur Andersen, and specifically its Houston office. During 2000, Arthur Andersen earned $25 million in audit fees and $27 million in consulting fees from Enron. The auditor's shoddy reports and lack of expertise in reviewing Enron's derivatives, revenue statements, special entities, and other accounting practices were the result of the firm's priority being fee collection rather than professional rigor.

How about the Enron board of directors? Why didn't they see what was going on and step in to curb the madness?

On paper, Enron had a respected board of directors comprised predominantly of outsiders with significant ownership stakes and a capable audit committee. Enron directors were highly paid for their services and financially tied to the company. In 2001, the average Enron director was paid nearly $400,000 in cash and stock, using the value of Enron stock on the date of its annual meeting.

Four hundred thousand dollars is the same salary paid to the president of the United States. And unlike that of an Enron director, the presidency is a full-time job.

The board members were easily manipulated by Fastow.

In the end, Enron investors lost $74 billion in the four years leading up to its bankruptcy, and its employees lost billions in pension benefits. Lay, Skilling, Fastow, and others were sentenced to prison.

While Enron was perhaps the most spectacular case of corporate fraud, the reality is that executive leaders in companies large and small face enormous pressure to perform. (In all fairness, sometimes the CEO is the primary instigator, as we saw in the case of Elizabeth Holmes, chairwoman and CEO of Theranos, who was convicted in 2022 of four counts of fraud that carried a maximum sentence of 20 years behind bars.)

As the Lucid Leader, you need to be on guard against the pressure that may be exerted on you by the board and investors to deliver the news they want to hear rather than the news that's real. You also need to be careful that you—either deliberately or without thinking—do not put pressure on your CFO to do the same.

You might say, "I'm a Lucid Leader. I play it straight and I don't like fabricated numbers. But certain board members are hard-liners. They don't care. They want what they want, and if they're not happy, they may fire me."

Yes, it's true that some boards and investors are single-minded and don't understand the realities of our hyper-competitive world. But whose fault is that? If you're a founder of your company, you have some control over whom you accept as an investor or board member. You can be lucid and you can demand they are the same. In the first years of Amazon, Jeff Bezos had a handful of investors, including his parents; in all, about 20 investors ponied up checks of about $50,000 apiece, for a total seed stage investment of around $1 million. In exchange, those combined investors got about 20 percent of the company. In June 1996, Amazon raised an $8 million Series A from Kleiner Perkins, its only VC investment before going public in May 1997. The IPO raised $54 million, giving the company a market value of $438 million.

The company grew incredibly quickly, and its investors didn't mind that it didn't report a profit until the fourth quarter of 2001. Bezos, his investors, and his board were all equally lucid about the company's growth strategy.

If you're brought into an existing company from the outside, and particularly a company that has a powerful and well-entrenched board, then you need to be super-lucid about what you're getting into. Now *you're* the candidate being interviewed for the job, and it's incredibly tempting to tell the board members what you think they want to hear.

This is what Herbert Deiss, former CEO and board chairman of the automotive giant Volkswagen AG, found out the hard way.

Crossed Signals at VW

Dr. Herbert Diess had a respected career in the German auto industry, including a tenure at BMW AG for over fifteen years. At Volkswagen, he was appointed chairman of the Board of Management of the Volkswagen Passenger Cars brand and Volkswagen Aktiengesellschaft. In 2018 he was named one of the "Best CEOs in the World" by the *CEOWORLD* magazine. The following year he was named VW Group CEO.

On July 20, 2022, the company announced that Diess was out. Why? He had ostensibly displeased members of the Porsche family (sometimes called Porsche–Piëch family), the prominent Austrian–German family of industrialists descended from the Austrian–German automotive pioneer Ferdinand Porsche. Its members control Porsche SE with 100 percent voting rights and have a 53.1 percent majority voting right over Volkswagen AG.

According to a report in the German magazine *Automobilwoche*, Diess "had been getting on the families' nerves for a long time." Diess struggled to muster broad support to execute his 89 billion euro ($91 billion) electric-vehicle and software strategy. This and the accusation that Porsche and

Audi jeopardized the company's Cariad software development unit with their need for special requests upset the Porsche family.[1]

What can the Lucid Leader learn from this?

As the employee of the VW board, and specifically the controlling Porsche family members, Diess needed to cultivate a culture of *two-way lucidity*. He didn't. The Porsche family had its own priorities, and Diess had his. There was a failure of lucidity on both sides.

Two-Way Lucidity

Unless you own and control your company 100 percent (which would make you a super-sole proprietor), while you may be the chief executive, you're going to be reporting to your board and investors or owners. You can be as lucid as you want, but if the lucidity isn't shared, or if your counterparts don't see things the same way you do, then there are going to be crossed signals and conflict. When that happens, and it's serious, it's the CEO who gets shown the door.

But the ball is always in your court. You control what you tell your board about the performance of the company.

You may be tempted to tell them only good news. You may think, "Why not make them happy? If there's bad news, we can fix it before the next board meeting." This is extremely dangerous, because you're being dishonest and because the problem you're hiding may only get worse.

You may be tempted to present a litany of complaints and doom-and-gloom, thinking that every little victory will then be celebrated even more. This is equally dangerous because the board may conclude that you're incompetent.

Two-way lucidity—the exchange of truth—builds trust and strengthens your relationship to your board. You need them to believe you, and you also need them to pitch in and help when necessary.

Here's how to ensure your relationship with your board is based on reality and mutual respect.

1. **Remember the Lucid Leader Manifesto:**

The Lucid Leader

- Is honest about himself or herself.
- Sees the world as it is, without preconceptions.
- Pursues the mission of the organization.
- Strives to make a positive impact on the world.

Every word you say to your board needs to be in alignment with these principles. Be honest, don't put a "spin" on bad news, and treat your board members like they're intelligent, caring people. If you have one board member who's a "problem child," just bite your tongue and say as little as possible. Remember: if a board member seems obnoxious to you, it's guaranteed he or she is obnoxious to the other board members as well.

2. **Tell them the most important news.** Board meetings can easily become bogged down in minutiae. The board chair needs to control this tendency, but sometimes they don't. Individual investors and board members probably don't know any more about your company and your market than you. As the CEO, it's your job to make sure your board promptly and succinctly knows about important items. If a website defect harms your relationship with customers, or a competitor makes an out-of-nowhere acquisition offer, tell your board chair ASAP, not next month. It doesn't build trust when they find out from elsewhere.

3. **Tell them your biggest challenges.** Board members do not need to know about the everyday problems that you get paid to fix. They need to know about serious issues that their expertise might be able to solve. Ask them for advice and come up with an action plan together of how you will try to solve it. Outside of regular meetings, figure out what you want advice on, then seek

out the board member who is most qualified to offer advice on that topic.

4. **Ask them to plan ahead.** One of the most important functions of a board is long-range planning. Share with them your vision and ask them for theirs. Be sure to iron out any differences while you're still in the talking phase. Aside from policing and oversight functions, the primary place directors can add value is in offering a different perspective on the competitive environment and the changes in that environment.

5. **Ensure you're on the same page.** Start with a conversation about shared values between yourself and your board members that includes such expectations as open-mindedness, accountability, financial stewardship, transparency, and confidentiality.

6. **Don't be the board chair.** It's become common in the United States for the CEO to also serve as the board chair. This is a bad idea. The same person can't do both jobs. Because an important part of the board's job is to evaluate the performance of the CEO from the point of view of the shareholders, it's a conflict of interest and the immediate result will be a loss of lucidity.

How to Choose Your Investors

Choose your investors? To many entrepreneurs, this may seem like a crazy idea! They would think, "Hey, if some Silicon Valley venture capitalist wanted to drop a couple of million dollars into my company, I'd be a fool to say 'no'!"

Not so fast!

The Lucid Leader knows that the type and size of investments, and the conditions under which they are offered, can either save or sink a company.

In a perfect world, every business could self-finance, and the owners wouldn't need to worry about repaying a loan or dealing with equity investors. But in the real world, businesses often need cash, usually to expand, continue research, or pay for a big purchase order that will produce revenue down the road.

Three types of funding are possible.

1. **Debt.** This means you take out a cash loan from a bank or private lender. You promise to repay the loan over a certain period of time. The lender is not entitled to any ownership percentage—they take their profit from the interest they charge or from a royalty on each item sold. If you don't repay the loan, they can sue you or foreclose on your company.

   As long as you make your payments on time, the financier has no control over your business. The interest you pay is tax-deductible. Once you've repaid the loan, your relationship with the lender ends.

   It's easy to forecast debt expenses because loan payments do not fluctuate over time. From a perspective of pure risk, lower ratios (0.4 or lower) of income to debt are considered better. Since the interest on a debt must be paid regardless of business profitability, if cash flow dries up, even temporarily, too much debt may compromise the business. Companies unable to service their own debt may be forced to sell off assets or declare bankruptcy.

2. **Equity.** Here, the investor provides funds in exchange for partial ownership of the company. They get paid back either through profit distributions or when they sell their shares.

   The only way to remove investors is to buy them out, but that's likely to be more expensive than the money they originally gave you.

   The more cash the investor provides, the more equity they want. If the investor ends up owning 51 percent of the company, you are now effectively their employee.

3. **Crowdfunding.** For smaller ventures, crowdfunding is a quasi-charitable method with a multitude of variations. In 1885, the Statue of Liberty was completed thanks to a crowdfunding campaign spearheaded by publisher Joseph Pulitzer. While

many of today's crowdfunding campaigns are for projects related to blockchain technology, one of the biggest crowdfunding campaigns is the U-Haul Investors Club, in which participants buy "U-Notes" to invest in U-Haul assets such as trucks and trailers. As of August 2022, the amount invested was over $194 million. AMERCO, the parent company, makes it clear that when you purchase a U-Note, you are lending money to AMERCO, which repays that loan by making scheduled repayments to you through the U-Haul Investors Club.

For the Lucid Leader, when choosing the type of funding you need, there are two cardinal rules: never give up majority stake in your company, and never take on debt that you're not certain you can repay.

Lucid Business Reports

Just as the Lucid Leader must *perceive* the world with objectivity, so must he or she *communicate* with transparency in all business matters. This includes all communications with investors, regulators, and the general public. By being transparent, the leader will build and reinforce his or her reputation for honesty.

Quarterly earnings reports are a common area where deceptive leaders seek to bury bad news while finding ready audiences for half-truths. One trick that unethical leaders frequently use is to release negative information after the close of the market on a Friday afternoon, especially when heading into a holiday weekend. Or a company might announce their lackluster earnings after hours when there is typically a lower level of investor attention being paid, or on a day when there are hundreds of other companies reporting and analysts are distracted.

The Lucid Leader knows that for investors, *less information* means *less certainty* and *higher risk*. When financial statements are not transparent, investors can't accurately determine a company's real fundamentals and level of risk. Complex, vaguely worded reports may also obscure the company's debt level, which is what Enron did. If a company hides its debt, investors can't estimate their exposure to bankruptcy risk.

A company's prospects for growth are related to how it invests. It's difficult to evaluate a company's investment performance if its investments are tucked away in holding companies and hidden from view.

Peloton's Endless Transparency Woes

In customer relations, a lack of lucidity can be very damaging. Consider the case of Peloton Interactive, the global maker of stationary bike exercise devices.

The Peloton Public Relations Disaster Tour first hit the road in December 2019 with a TV spot that made Vox.com proclaim, "Peloton's terrifying new ad is the best horror movie in recent memory." The spot, named internally "The Gift That Gives Back," featured a very fit young woman whose male partner gives her a special holiday present: a shiny new Peloton, so that she could become even *more* fit in order to please him. The tag line was, "Give them a gift that goes beyond the holiday season. Give the gift of Peloton." The creepy ad reminded many of an updated Grimm's fairy tale, where the beautiful young maiden spins and spins, all to please the handsome prince.[2]

Still, Peloton was riding high. On December 24, 2020—it was Christmas Eve, suggesting a boom in Covid-19 lockdown holiday gift sales—the company's stock price hit an all-time high of $162.72.

From there, it was downhill all the way, as blunder after blunder slammed the company.

In May 2021, after one child had died after being pulled under the treadmill while a parent was running on the Tread+ Peloton treadmill, and almost 40 others sustained injuries, including fractured bones, the U.S. Consumer Product Safety Commission warned people with children and pets to immediately stop using the product. Peloton initially rejected the agency's request to recall the product and instead warned parents to keep children away from the treadmill, before it relented and voluntarily recalled the Tread and Tread+ products.

In July 2021, a New York City couple filed a lawsuit against the company claiming their three-year-old son suffered third-degree burns after being trapped under the treadmill. Peloton persisted with various fixes, but the steady drip-drip of bad publicity took its toll.

The company became the butt of jokes. In December 2021, on the TV show *And Just Like That . . .* , the character of Mr. Big (played by Chris Noth) had a heart attack and died after riding a Peloton bike. Several weeks later, an episode of the show *Billions* featured a character likewise suffering a heart attack after using a Peloton device.

Then came "Project Tinman," an internal operation that sought to conceal signs of rust and corrosion on the company's stationary exercise bikes manufactured in Taiwan before shipping the bikes to customers who had already paid for them. The company hoped to avoid another major product recall because of the rust.

In January 2022, CNBC reported, citing internal company documents, that Peloton had a massive inventory of unsold bikes and treadmills, causing it to pause production. The company denied the report.

The following month, the company announced that it would be laying off about 2,800 employees (20 percent of its corporate workforce) and would suspend construction of its new production factory called Peloton Output Park, which was expected to create around 2,000 new jobs for the company. In July, the company announced to employees it would cut nearly 800 jobs and begin outsourcing some roles and positions.

"These are hard choices because we are impacting people's lives," Barry McCarthy, Peloton's chief executive, wrote in a memo to employees and reported by the *New York Times*. "These changes are essential if Peloton is ever going to become cash-flow positive."[3]

The moral of the story is that not only must you, the leader, be lucid in how you perceive yourself, your company, and the market, but that it must be a two-way street. You must be transparent and open with your investors, employees, and customers. No one likes a company that seems secretive or has a creepy agenda. When analysts and ordinary investors look at a company and see a string of public relations disasters, the risk meter gets pinned in the red. There are countless companies where investors large and small can park their money, so why should they choose one that makes elementary missteps?

Don't get caught up in your own hype. It's cool to make products that are super high-tech, but when you start thinking your product has become mythological, it's time to step back and say, "We're here to serve our customers, and we're grateful for every single one of them."

Take Action!

- ✓ As the CEO, you're not at the very top of the organizational pyramid. You're occupying a spot on the Circle of Accountability. Your Lucid Leadership must impact your investors and board members as well as your subordinates.
- ✓ Maintain close communication with the board chair and other board members who are active. Encourage them to be lucid as well, and try to tamp down unrealistic or "pie in the sky" notions.
- ✓ Focus the board on long-range planning, not short-term micromanaging.
- ✓ Lucidity is a two-way street. See the world clearly, and let the world see *you* clearly.

5

Customers

Imagine your organization is like a ship on the open ocean. (Admittedly it's a familiar literary device, but in this case, none other works better.) You, the captain, know yourself and your capabilities. You know your strengths and weaknesses, and to assist you, you've thoughtfully chosen top officers who complement your abilities and compensate for your liabilities. Your crew is well trained and loyal. You carry a valuable cargo to a distant port, where your buyer awaits.

As far as you, your ship, and your crew are concerned, you're entirely lucid, and headed for success.

Not so fast!

Unfortunately, you must deal with the real world. In your case, the real world has brought you a massive fog bank, wild winds, and raging seas. (All at once—impossible but true!) Are you on course? Is a big storm approaching? Are there pirate ships lurking over the horizon, ready to pounce when you're preoccupied with other problems?

If you are not clearly seeing through the chaos and disruption of the external environment, you have little chance of guiding your vessel safely to its destination.

Your Customers Demand—and Get—More

The accelerating pace of technology is having a direct effect on the expectations of consumers. More than ever, they demand what they want and they expect to get it quickly.

Amazon is the poster child for this revolution. Before Jeff Bezos founded the company in his garage in 1994, if you wanted to buy a consumer item you had two choices:

You could get in your car and drive to the store. It might be local shop, a big-box Walmart, or a shopping mall. In fact, the end of the twentieth century was the Golden Age of the Mall. The biggest, the Mall of America, opened in 1992 with 5.6 million square feet under its huge roof. The mega-mall was the future of retail—until suddenly it wasn't.

Your second choice was to either phone the store on your landline or order by snail mail. At the store or warehouse, an employee would eventually get around to packing and shipping your order. The phrase "Please allow 2–3 weeks for delivery" was standard operating procedure.

This was how it had been for centuries: either go to the store yourself, or order and wait for delivery.

Amazon, aided and abetted by the newly emerging internet, exploded that system. Suddenly, consumers could seamlessly order products from a website and have them delivered the next day. Many of the big physical stores, like Walmart, saw disruption on the horizon and ramped up their own internet marketing programs. Sales pages became personalized, with a "Hello, Susan" message when Susan logged on, where she'd see a list of books or other products the algorithm decided Susan would like. From the start, Bezos visualized Amazon not as merely an online bookstore but as a way of gathering marketing data on affluent, educated shoppers. In order to increase sales volume and get more consumer data, the books were priced close to cost. After collecting information on millions of customers, Amazon was ready to sell anything at rock-bottom prices on the Internet.

It took Amazon only a decade to disrupt the traditional book business. Borders Group declared bankruptcy in 2011. And it wasn't just bookstores that felt the sting of the new internet businesses: K-B Toys closed in 2009, and Toys-R-Us shuttered in 2017 and 2018. Travel agents have become a relic of the past and are now a niche luxury provider. Printed encyclopedias including *Britannica* and *The World Book* are gone.

As consumers flock to the most convenient and accessible choices, entire industries face destruction.

The golden age of the shopping mall peaked in the late 1990s—just before internet retail exploded. For malls, it's been downhill ever since. According to Fundera, since 2001, online sales have grown by 300 percent, while department store sales have dropped by 50 percent. A 2017 Credit Suisse report estimated that one in four U.S. malls would close by 2022. During the decline, a new term emerged: "dead mall." No, it's not a Stephen King novel. A dead mall—also known as a zombie mall or ghost mall—is a shopping mall with many empty stores. Malls are considered "dead" (for the purposes of leasing) when they have no surviving anchor store that could attract foot traffic to the mall. With no big anchor store, the smaller interior stores wither and die.

Telephone landlines are vanishing. In New York City in the year 2000, about 30,000 public pay phones dotted the sidewalks of every block. Then they began to disappear. On May 23, 2022, at the corner of Seventh Avenue and West 50th Street, a crane removed the city's very last public pay phone. There are no more.

Print newspapers and magazines are a shadow of what they once were. This includes porn magazines; online porn is now a multi-billion-dollar industry. Physical road maps—you used to buy them everywhere—are gone.

All of these technologies, and more, were supported by successful businesses. Many of these businesses vanished, while the agile ones adapted and survived or even thrived. Take *Playboy*, for instance. The iconic girlie magazine founded by Hugh Hefner in 1953 published its final paper copy in March 2020. To many, it seemed like a relic of a bygone age, hopelessly outgunned by the videos found online. But today, PLBY Group Inc. (NASDAQ, PLBY) operates three highly successful business categories: direct-to-consumer sales of third-party products through its owned-and-operated e-commerce platforms; licensing of Playboy brands to third parties; and digital subscription and content, including the sale of subscriptions to Playboy programming and trademark licensing for online gaming products. It turns out the Playboy brand has tremendous market value; in 2019, Playboy ranked number 21 among the Top 150 Global Licensors by *License Global* magazine, and accounts for of half of the company's revenue. (Number one on the list? You guessed it—the Walt Disney Company.)[1]

Increasingly, consumers can get the exact product they want, customized expressly for them. For example, in July 2021, the Ford Motor Company announced it was moving away from the business model of having customers choose a car from inventory at the dealership to ordering the exact car they wanted online, and then picking it up. "I know we are wasting money on incentives," said CEO Jim Farley. "We are really committed to going to an order-based system and keeping inventories at 50 to 60 days' supply." Earlier in 2021, Ford introduced Ford Express Buy, an online-only way to purchase a Ford vehicle in the United States. "It's a really exciting way for us to sell vehicles in partnership with our dealers," said Ford's president of the Americas and International Markets Group, Kumar Galhotra. "You can start building your vehicle, pricing it, put it in the cart, and you can go all the way to make a transaction. Ford Credit can approve the customer's credit in seconds, and you can make the payment and the dealer can deliver the car to your home."[2]

But wait—what about the traditional test drive? Ford's research revealed that customers are less interested in taking the car for a spin around the block. They know they can return the car if they don't like it, and let's face it—most regular family cars all feel the same to drive. It's like books, when Jeff Bezos realized that most people don't need to handle a book before they buy it.

Your Customers Have a Big Voice!

Not only have consumers come to expect a robust selection of products delivered with unprecedented speed, they also have acquired a greater voice in expressing their preferences and judgments about what you offer them.

In the old days—the twentieth century—consumers "voted with their pocketbooks." This meant that if you offered a product or service, and you projected your sales for, say, the next quarter, you would know if your product or service was a success if you hit your projection by the end of the quarter. If you fell short, it meant *something was wrong*.

But *what* was wrong? What was it that made consumers reject what you offered?

It could have been the price. Maybe it was too expensive. Or perhaps you underestimated the need or desire for your product. There may have been a design flaw or a quality control issue. Maybe it was the wrong color!

True, you had customer surveys. These happened after the fact, when it was too late.

Focus groups were useful but limited in their real-life application.

Meanwhile, from the point of view of the customer, there was no sense of a "customer community." If you had a problem with the product, you called the company or wrote a letter of complaint. You had no way of knowing if the shortcoming in your product was felt by others, or if you were the only one with a gripe. If the company treated you poorly, you had no platform to voice a complaint to your fellow consumers.

Today, thanks to digital communications, consumers wield tremendous power. A consumer can make his or her complaint in the digital public square (DPS), where everyone can read it. Strictly speaking, the original Digital Public Square project grew out of the Munk School's Global Dialogue on the Future of Iran, a project that began in May of 2013. The term has grown to include any user-driven website offering user-generated content (UGC) created by a community of people with a common interest. For consumers, they include Amazon Customer Reviews, Angie's List, Trustpilot, TripAdvisor, Yelp, Foursquare, and dozens more.

You never know what a consumer will post on a review site! After less than a minute of poking around on Yelp, I found this priceless gem, directed at an electrical contractor. This is the entire one-star review: "Haven't use their service but just saw one of their employees driving a company truck, drinking and driving. So that might be a good reason to avoid this company."

Ouch!

Here's another blistering review of a moving company: "These scammers change company names and remove their Yelp listing before negative information catches up with them. . . . They deserve to be OUT OF BUSINESS and management IMPRISONED for all of their impropriety. Keywords: fraud, shakedown, extortion, theft, racket, stealing, scum, scam."

Yikes!

Obviously, your company would never do anything so terrible as to deserve a review like that one. But here's the thing: angry or just plain crazy customers are far more likely to post a review than customers who are pleasantly pleased. You may have a thousand happy customers and one unhappy one . . . and guess who's going to go to the DPS and yell about it? That's right, the unhappy one. This is why you need to stay on top of your social media presence so you can counterbalance the inevitable negative comments with positive responses. But more about that later in the book.

The Market Analysis

The fundamental tool of external lucidity is the market analysis. Whether your company is B2C or B2B, product or service, the number one question you must answer is, "Do we have something the market wants and will pay for?"

This may seem like a no-brainer, but it's a big reason why many companies fail. There are two primary reasons why your product or service might not sell:

1. **The market is saturated.** While some "first adapter" consumers will try any new product just because it's new, they will not provide the growth you need to survive. Either you need to sell into a small but exclusive market—think supercars or megayachts—or you need to sell in volume to a broad market. Either way, your product needs to differentiate itself from the competition. This requires that you know the competition. You have to know their products, prices, level of quality, and availability to consumers, and you have to see an opening where your product fills a gap.

   Sometimes physical proximity can be enough of a differentiator, especially for restaurants. For example, in the United States in 2022, the Subway restaurant chain had 21,000 locations. Worldwide, it boasted 37,000 locations. You might think that the last thing America needs is another Subway store! Yet if a neighborhood lacks a Subway location, and the nearest one is far enough away to not be a direct competitor, you can be sure a franchisee will open one there.

2. **The market doesn't need the product.** A classic example of an intriguing innovation that found no market was the ill-fated Segway PT. At its public unveiling in 2001, inventor Dean Kamen promised the Segway—the two-wheeled self-balancing vehicle that used computerized gyroscopes to allow standing riders to travel by shifting their body weight—"will be to the car what the car was to the horse and buggy." Within a year, he projected the Segway factory would be cranking out 10,000 machines a week and make $12 billion in sales. That never happened. Why not? The machine was too expensive, too heavy, and its batteries limited its range. It was also *dangerous.* In 2010, UK entrepreneur Jimi Heselden—who'd just bought the troubled Segway Corporation—was killed on his Yorkshire estate when he drove his Segway off a cliff.

In 2015, Segway was acquired by Ninebot Inc., a Beijing-based transportation robotics startup. Five years later, Ninebot ceased production of the Segway PT and laid off the 21 employees working at the Bedford, New Hampshire, plant. Only 140,000 units were sold during the lifetime of the product, and in the later years the Segway PT made up only 1.5 percent of total company profit. Today, Segway-Ninebot manufactures and sells a wide variety of conventional electric personal vehicles.

A market analysis is a thorough assessment of a market within a specific industry. It includes the dynamics of the market and growth potential, volume and value, potential customer segments, buying patterns, competition, and other important factors. A thorough marketing analysis should answer the following questions:

- Who are my potential customers?
- How many potential customers are there?
- Is my product in alignment with what they want?
- How much are customers willing to pay for my product?

- What are my customers' buying habits?
- Who are my main competitors?
- What are their strengths and weaknesses?

The Funhouse Mirror World of Market Research

Leaders who fancy themselves to be visionaries like Steve Jobs often cite his comments on his lack of use of market research. Jobs famously said to *Fortune* magazine, "We do no market research. We don't hire consultants. The only consultants I've ever hired in my ten years is one firm to analyze Gateway's retail strategy so I would not make some of the same mistakes they made [when launching Apple's retail stores]. But we never hire consultants, per se. We just want to make great products."

And he told *Businessweek*, "It's really hard to design products by focus groups. A lot of times, people don't know what they want until you show it to them."

These remarks have been misused by reckless entrepreneurs who have embraced the concept of "fail fast"—you design a product, rush it to market, and if it flops, you cancel it quickly.

What's a Lucid Leader to do? Sometimes the world of market research looks more like you're wandering through the funhouse mirror ride at the theme park. What's real? What's an illusion?

To get back to Apple, in fact they do plenty of market research.

In 1997, Jobs spoke to attendees of the Apple Worldwide Developers Conference where he clearly stated that customers must be placed at the center of operations: "One of the things I've always found is that you've got to start with the customer experience and work backwards to the technology." He then added that the questions Apple asks are, "What incredible benefits can we give to the customer? Where can we take the customer?"[3]

They may not do focus groups, which asks consumers to speculate on the future, but they do consumer surveys. Apple takes great pains to understand the needs of their customers, and surveys them to supplement their own internal data and thinking. This came to light in 2012 when, during a legal conflict with Samsung, the company's VP of product marketing submitted a document to the court explaining why documents relating to Apple's market research (specifically iPhone surveys) should be kept secret. One was an "iPhone Owner Study" labeled "Apple Market Research & Analysis, May 2011." It surveyed users in multiple countries about why they bought an iPhone. (As it turned out, "Trust in the Apple brand" was number one.)

Feedback surveys have proven to be an effective way for Apple to gather customer insights. The company emails surveys to customers immediately after they have made a purchase. Customers are asked to rate their satisfaction level and how likely they are to purchase again.

The Four Key Axioms of Customer Surveys

Just like employee surveys, customer surveys can be very helpful (as we'll see in the pages ahead), but sadly, most of them are unreliable and annoy the customer. They ask irrelevant questions, such as your age. They ask too many questions and make the customer feel like an unpaid employee or a lab rat. They're designed to elicit praise and avoid pain.

The RealRatings approach—developed after years of experience in the trenches with both spunky startups and global corporations—is different. It follows the four key axioms of customer surveys, and provides the Lucid Leader with actionable, accurate information.

1. Keep It Simple

Your customer is giving you their time, and their time is valuable.

The #1 rule of voluntary customer surveys, where you ask the customer without any forewarning, "Please take our survey," is that *it must be brief.* With just a handful of multiple-choice questions, it must take the customer no longer than two minutes to complete.

If you try to detain them too long, you'll lose them. In an OpinionLab study, 52 percent of respondents indicated they would likely abandon a survey after just three minutes. Even if people make it past three minutes, the quality of their survey responses declines as the respondent hurries through to the end. Keeping your questions brief and simple to understand is the best way to combat this kind of response fatigue.[4]

2. Ask Relevant, Actionable Questions

Because your survey is short, the questions must be important and the answers actionable. If you ask, "Would you buy another product from us?" the answer means *nothing*. If the customer says "no," what are you going to do? You have no idea *why* the customer is unhappy, so what can you improve? Price? Quality? Service? The smell of the store?

Surveys should be narrow. You cannot hope to learn everything from a survey, so you need to decide exactly what you want to know about. Then after a period of time, you change the survey to address other potential problems.

3. Look for the Hatepoints

Most traditional surveys are designed to elicit positive responses. Customers often try to be polite and tell the survey sponsors what they think the sponsors want to hear. The results are bland mush.

Asking customers what they *hated* about their interaction with your brand can be scary! No one wants to hear bad news. But it's a bedrock principle of Lucid Leadership. Sure, if compelled to name something they hated about their experience, they may say something silly. But more often than not, you'll get a golden nugget of information that will help your company improve.

Remember the Golden Rule of Retail:

The customer wants exactly what they envision. They want it now. They want it at the lowest possible price.

You need to know in what ways you are *falling short* of meeting this ideal state.

4. Give Your Customer a Reward

When you ask a customer to participate in a survey, you're asking them to provide two things of value—their time and their opinion. You don't give away products for free, so why should your customers give you free stuff? Reward them with a discount, a gift card, entry into a sweepstake, or something else that's easy and fun.

The Next Level:
The RealRatings Customer Survey

Earlier in this book, we used the four customer personas—the Driver, Analytical, Amiable, and Collaborative—to help construct our employee survey. The breakthrough idea was that to be truly effective, a survey needed to adapt itself to the *expectations of the consumer*. Of course, you can say that every consumer wants the best possible product at the lowest possible price, delivered ASAP. But the *process* by which the consumer *discovers* and *chooses* the product can vary greatly. This means that from one consumer to another, their expectations of the process can be very different.

The Driver knows what she wants and expects prompt, efficient, no-nonsense service. She isn't looking for friendship and will quickly pile on the hate if her expectations are not met.

The Analytical needs to know every detail of the product or service. Think about the person who goes to a restaurant and, before ordering the salmon, interrogates the server about the country of origin of the salmon, if it were wild caught or sustainably farm raised, and if it had been fed processed meal? That's the Analytical.

The Amiable wants you to approve of their purchase of the product or service. They expect a high level of personal service. An Amiable will spend half an hour chatting on the phone with the Zappos customer service rep before ordering one pair of shoes.

The Collaborator needs the consensus of a group or partner in order to proceed. The collaborator is the person who will say, "I like it, but I need to talk to my partner before we buy."

Of course there are shades of each—for example, a Collaborator may show some characteristics of the Amiable—but as a general concept, the system hits the mark.

These types each view your company through their own eyes. If asked to describe the sales staff at your company, the Analytical might say, "Their sales team is highly informative. They really know their products." The Driver might say, "The salespeople take care of business quickly and efficiently." The Collaborator appreciates your patience and lack of pressure while he consults with his partner. The Amiable might say your staff is exceptionally friendly and welcoming ("They serve you free coffee and doughnuts.")

And guess what? They're all talking about the same sales staff! It's because customer-facing employees have been trained to adapt their behavior to match or mirror that of the customer. They know how to pivot to meet the expectation of each customer persona.

The Qualifying Question

The first question you ask of your customer will qualify them into one of the four customer types. (Again, this is an example. Your company may need more than four.) For example, for a store called Millie's Fashions, the first four survey questions could be this:

1. When I came to Millie's Fashions, I wanted to:
   A. Make my purchase as quickly and efficiently as possible.
   B. Take time to explore the store and get to know its staff.
   C. Learn all I could about the item before I bought it, such as where it was made.
   D. Have the opportunity to consult with my partner.

Because this is just a qualifying round, the respondent can be asked to choose the one that's closest to what they expected. This will ensure just one choice.

Survey for the Amiable

Based on their choice, the respondent is then presented with one of four different surveys. The survey presented to Drivers will be different from the survey presented to Amiables, Analyticals, and Collaborators. The survey presented to Amiables will focus not only on the ubiquitous questions of product quality, but on questions designed to measure to what extent the company scored lovepoints and/or hatepoints based on their specific expectations.

After the initial qualifying question or questions, the respondent is asked to answer two sets of questions. There should be no more than five in each set, for a maximum number of questions set at 10, plus the initial qualifying question.

In the first set of five questions, the Amiable respondent is asked what she loved about the experience. In the second set of five questions, she's asked about what she disliked. We *want her* to tell us something she hated. The love-hate sequence goes like this:

1. **Lovepoints.** Using the scale of 1 (unliked), 2 (liked), 3 (loved), or 4 (really loved), please indicate your level of *happiness* with the following five events:

   A. My interaction with the first salesperson I spoke to when I entered the store.

   B. My interaction with the salesperson who rang up my purchase.

   C. How long I had to wait in line to pay.

   D. Learning about the store's returns policy.

   E. The overall vibe of the store staff. Do they seem like nice people?

2. **Hatepoints.** Using the scale of 1 (not good), 2 (bad), 3 (hated), or 4 (really hated), please indicate your level of *dissatisfaction* with the following five events:

   A. How long I had to wait before a salesperson greeted me.

   B. The time spent looking for the item I wanted.

   C. Having my questions answered by the salesperson.

   D. The checkout process.

   E. The level of attentiveness of the salesperson to me and what I wanted.

As you can see, the questions presented in the two parts are similar but not exactly the same. They are primarily focused on what's important to the Amiable, which is her interaction with the staff. The reason we ask specifically for what the customer may have hated was to give the customer "permission" to express her true feelings. We're asking her what she didn't like about her experience, and we want her to tell us.

Survey for the Driver

In the first set of five questions, the Driver is asked what he or she loved about the experience based on the criteria most important to them. In the second set of five questions, they're asked about what they hated. The love-hate sequence goes like this:

1. **Lovepoints**. Using the scale of 1 (unliked), 2 (liked), 3 (loved), or 4 (really loved), please indicate your level of *happiness* with the following five events:
   A. The layout of the store and ease of navigation.
   B. My interaction with the first salesperson I spoke to when I entered the store.
   C. How quickly I was able to locate the product I wanted.
   D. How long I had to wait in line to pay.
   E. The overall vibe of the store staff. Is the operation highly efficient?

2. **Hatepoints.** Using the scale of 1 (not good), 2 (bad), 3 (hated), or 4 (really hated), please indicate your level of *dissatisfaction* with the following five events:
   A. The time it took me to buy the product I wanted.
   B. The exact match of what I wanted versus what was available to buy.
   C. Having my questions promptly answered by the salesperson.
   D. The price of my purchase relative to my expectations.
   E. The overall "hassle-free" nature of my experience.

The questions presented in the two parts are similar but not exactly the same. They are focused on what's important to the Driver, which is his or her ability to get in and out of the store quickly and with the product they want. We ask what the customer hated to give them "permission" to express their true feelings.

Could a single survey be designed that would capture the same information from each of the four customer types? Probably, but it would be exceedingly long. Few customers—and absolutely no Drivers!—would be willing to take the time to complete a long survey. Eleven questions—the qualifier and the two pairs of five each—are about as much as most people will be willing to give you. Anything longer will get you a right rate of non-completion and careless answers.

Take Action!

- ✓ Know your market! Don't guess. Don't fancy yourself to be another Steve Jobs who can peer into a crystal ball and see the future. (He couldn't, and you can't either.) A smart market analysis will tell you if consumer (B2C) or another business (B2B) would want to pay money for your product or service.
- ✓ You must ensure that you're serving your customers in the way they expect. Make it as easy as possible for them to buy from you! For example, when you want to order a pizza from Domino's, there are 15 different ways (at last count) you can do it. How does your sales system measure up?
- ✓ The Lucid Leader has his or her finger on the pulse of customer opinion. Your marketing people need to monitor and respond to Amazon Customer Reviews, Angie's List, Trustpilot, TripAdvisor, Yelp, Foursquare, and any other digital platform where your customers might either praise or condemn your company.
- ✓ The RealRatings approach follows the four key axioms of customer surveys, and provides the Lucid Leader with actionable, accurate information. The four axioms are:
  1. Keep it simple.
  2. Ask relevant, actionable questions.
  3. Look for the hatepoints.
  4. Give your customer a reward.
- ✓ The RealRatings Customer Survey measures how well you are meeting your customers' expectations, with

the understanding that different customer types have different expectations, and therefore should not be treated the same.

- The Driver knows what she wants and expects prompt, efficient, no-nonsense service.
- The Analytical needs to know every detail of the product or service.
- The Amiable wants to be your friend.
- The Collaborator needs the consensus of a group or partner in order to proceed.

✓ The Qualifying Question is critical. Using the same "skip logic" we used in the RealRatings Employee Survey, it guides the customer to the survey questions designed for him or her.

Lucid Leader Attribute #1: Integrous

In the first five chapters of this book, we've described the Lucid Leader, established the importance of Lucid Leadership in today's accelerating business environment, and shown how the Lucid Leader interacts with his or her world in four key directions: inwardly (toward the self), and outwardly toward their employees, customers, and investors and directors.

The goal is *perfect transparency in every direction*, with no preconceptions, biases, distorted thinking, or hidden agendas.

This transparency leads to *decisive, accurate decisions based on reality*. It produces agility and a rapid response to challenges. It greatly increases the odds that the decision made will be the correct one. It leaves the door open for strategic change.

The result is organizational growth, greater corporate value in the community, and an increase in return on investment.

The importance of lucidity in business cannot be overemphasized. The best analogy would be to a pilot of a fighter aircraft. In the early part of the twentieth century, a fighter plane might have traveled at 100 mph. That speed required a certain quickness of human reflexes. Over the years, speeds increased. Today's fighter pilots can travel at 1,600 mph or more. That's nearly a mile in two seconds. In three-dimensional airspace, he or she may be facing an opponent traveling at the same speed. To operate effectively, the pilot needs *instant and accurate information* from his plane and his environment. At those speeds, fractions of a second matter. Any distortion or garbling of information can spell disaster. Any false assumptions held by the pilot or his ground crew could be deadly.

Corporate leaders may not pilot supersonic jet fighters, but they guide complex organizations that impact the daily lives of employees and other stakeholders.

Having charted the terrain and described the flow of information to and from the leader, the next question is, "What are the personal characteristics of the Lucid Leader? Can such a person be developed, either with training or with a program of self-improvement?"

Lucid Leaders are individuals whom people want to follow. People want to follow them because they respect their integrity, expertise, and confidence. They are very clear on what they stand for and the goals they hope to achieve. They focus their effort on things that really matter, and because they are clear on all aspects of who they are and what they stand for, they attract the very best employees, colleagues, partners, and investors.

How do we define and recognize the Lucid Leader whom everyone admires and wants to support? In my work with global executives—both lucid and those aspiring to be lucid—I've found the greatest leaders possess four attributes, which all come from a place of personal human clarity.

Those four key attributes are integrous, mission-centered, humanistic, and innovative.

Let's look at integrous.

Someone who is integrous has the quality of integrity. It's the quality of being honest and having strong moral principles. It's a firm adherence to a code of wholesome moral values. It's about being honest and not cheating anyone, and of being true to your word.

But what does it mean to the Lucid Leader in particular?

It means all of the above, but there's also a second meaning of the word, which is "to be whole and undivided." The word is derived from the Latin adjective "*integer*," meaning "whole" or "complete." It's defined as "an undivided or unbroken completeness," or "a state of being complete or whole."

In terms of the human personality, it means to be consistent in every situation, and to accept incoming information as objectively as possible without artificial coloration or the addition of bias.

It also carries the meaning that we often see in architecture or mechanical engineering, where we describe a building or a bridge as having "structural integrity." This means the structure has sufficient internal strength to withstand the natural forces to which it will be exposed, such as high winds or extreme temperatures. If a building lacks structural integrity, then it poses a danger of collapse and is a hazard. This is not a theoretical issue—it can have consequences in real life.

On the afternoon of June 24, 2021, Champlain Towers South, a 12-story beachfront condominium in the Miami suburb of Surfside, Florida, partially collapsed. Ninety-eight people died. The problems—revealed after the fact—included the long-term degradation of reinforced concrete structural support in the basement-level parking garage under the pool deck, due to water penetration and corrosion of the reinforcing steel.

There had been many warning signs.

In 2018, an inspection performed by the engineering firm Morabito Consultants identified a "major error" in the construction of the pool deck, whereby rainwater was allowed to collect rather than drain off. Over the years, this persistent moisture had severely damaged the concrete slabs below the pool deck. The report stated the waterproofing below the pool deck was beyond repair and needed to be completely removed and replaced.

In October 2020, repairs around the pool were suspended when engineers said the deterioration had penetrated so deeply that the work would have risked destabilizing that area.

In April 2021, two months before the collapse, a letter sent to residents noted that concrete deterioration was accelerating and had become "much worse" since the 2018 report, and outlined a $15-million remedial-works program.

In addition to the freshwater infiltrations from the defectively constructed pool deck, a maintenance manager had reported a possible excessive ingress of salt water, which can cause more aggressive spalling—that is, the rusting of rebar and the subsequent chipping off of chunks of weakened concrete.

The Surfside disaster was a type of progressive collapse, whereby one structural part gives way, destabilizing and removing support from other parts, which in turn collapse and rapidly remove structural support from the larger structure.

The same thing can happen to people. Over time, the structural weaknesses in the personality of a leader can be amplified to the extent that they threaten his or her good judgment, and can even lead to disaster.

Observers are often amazed when corporate leaders with impeccable resumes are revealed to be corrupt and deceitful crooks. But if you look closely at many of them, you'll often discover they have significant character flaws which they managed to conceal for years or even decades. Once firmly ensconced in the corner office with few controls on their behavior, they lose their integrity and succumb to greed.

The same hidden-character phenomenon may apply to bad CEOs. They may manage to keep their greed controlled while climbing the corporate ladder, but when they reach the top with no one but an often inattentive or easily intimidated board of directors to check them, their true personalities are revealed. History books are replete with examples of CEOs who lacked integrity—who were *criminal*—and yet, like the Surfside condo building, from the outside looked perfectly fine and even admirable: Enron's Kenneth Lay, WorldCom's Bernard Ebbers, Tyco's Dennis Kozlowski, Theranos's Elizabeth Holmes, and even the greatest Wall Street con artist of modern times, Bernie Madoff.

What does this mean to you, the Lucid Leader?

It means that if you choose to discard integrity and become an outlaw dedicated only to your own greed, then for a while, at least, *you can get away with it*. Yes, while eventually you'll trip up—they all do!—for a significant period of time you'll be able to pull the wool over everyone's eyes and pocket your ill-gotten gains.

Integrity Is a Personal Choice

This is the bottom line truth: Your personal integrity is a matter of *your own choice*. Human defects are even more difficult to detect than those in a condo building or a bridge. With the right inspections, issues of steel and concrete can be identified and acted upon. But the human soul is adept at hiding its secrets. Everyone of us is a skilled actor. (You don't think so? Recall the last time you met a woman wearing a hideous dress and you said to her with a smile, "How lovely you look tonight.")

Like a comic book superhero, the Lucid Leader must use his or her powers of clarity and insight with integrity and for the common good. It must be a conscious choice, because the ability to see clearly does not bring with it a moral component. Sharks have the ability to know every detail of their environment, and they have no moral integrity. Bernie Madoff—a sort of human shark—was not a stupid man. He was exceptionally intelligent and he knew the business of investing as well as anyone. His career began auspiciously. After graduating from Hofstra University in 1960 with a bachelor of arts degree in political science, he briefly attended law school but left after his first year to start his own company, Bernard L. Madoff Investment Securities, LLC. In order to compete with members of the New York Stock Exchange that had trading floor access, Madoff began using innovative computer information technology to disseminate its quotes. This technology eventually became NASDAQ, founded in 1971 as the world's first electronic stock market. Madoff's firm functioned as a third market trading provider, bypassing exchange specialist firms by directly executing orders over the counter from retail.

Madoff was not a reclusive person. He was well known on Wall Street, a prominent philanthropist who served on boards of nonprofit institutions, and active in the National Association of Securities Dealers (NASD), a self-regulatory securities-industry organization, where he served as chairman of its board of directors and member of its board of governors.

The first signs that Madoff had abandoned his professional integrity came in 1992, and again in 1999, but perhaps because of his personal popularity, nothing came of these foreshadowings. After he was arrested in 2008, Madoff told federal inspectors that he could have been caught five years earlier, but that incompetent investigators had "acted like Lt. Columbo" and never asked the right questions:

"I was astonished. They never even looked at my stock records. If investigators had checked with The Depository Trust Company, a central securities depository, it would've been easy for them to see. If you're looking at a Ponzi scheme, it's the first thing you do."

Just as there's no "lucidity test," there's no "integrity test" either. It has to come from within you. It has to be something you embrace because it's the right thing to do for yourself, your employees, your customers, and your community.

The Ancient Roots of Integrity

Earlier in this chapter I mentioned sharks. They have no integrity in the moral sense. They're very good at what they do, which is to hunt and eat other creatures of the sea, but they're totally self-centered. They know nothing except their own needs and survival.

We humans are different. Unlike individual sharks, which are quite capable of surviving alone in their environment and do not hunt cooperatively the way dolphins and killer whales do, human beings are utterly incapable of surviving alone. We are this way today and were equally vulnerable thousands of years ago. In our early days—*Homo sapiens* emerged about 160,000 years ago—to avoid being eaten by bigger, faster predators, we had to form defensive groups and job-sharing communities. To succeed by dividing tasks and protecting one another requires the four attributes of the Lucid Leader: integrous, mission-centered, humanistic, and innovative. If our hunter-gatherer ancestors, who lived in an environment where one miscalculation could mean death, did not possess the attributes of Lucid Leaders, they would not have lasted long. Information about the environment—the location of prey, available food, and predators—needed to be perceived correctly and then transmitted to the group accurately, with no "wishful thinking" or "false inflation of value." If exactly ten antelope were spotted, the report had to be precise. If berries were found that were edible and not poisonous, this information needed to be conveyed. If a snake were seen near the camp, it had to be identified correctly as venomous or harmless. Lives depended upon the accuracy of the reports.

We see this same need in today's military, especially during combat operations. For example, during the Iraq war, when a suspected enemy sniper was spotted in the window of a building, before the sniper was taken out by U.S. forces, the soldiers had to be *absolutely certain* that the target was indeed an enemy and not a friendly Iraqi or U.S. Marine. There was *no room for error*. The process of target identification and elimination had to have *absolute integrity*.

The same rules apply in healthcare settings. Physicians and those who are entrusted with the health and well-being of their constituents need to have the highest level of integrity. As the ancient Hippocratic Oath said, "I will keep pure and holy both my life and my art." Healthcare providers require accurate information about the patient and their condition, treatment options, risks, and likely outcomes. They're required to convey this information accurately and concisely to the patient.

When lives hang in the balance—whether thousands of years ago on the African savannah or in modern times on the battlefield or in the hospital—integrity, both personal and group, is mandatory. There can be no exceptions and no relaxing of standards.

Business Integrity

In business, integrity begins with you, the Lucid Leader, and needs to be present and robust in every area of the organization. It means operating with consistency in interactions at all levels, and representing the organization in an honest and consistent way to all stakeholders. To achieve business integrity, do these things:

- **Be honest.** Insist your employees are transparent in all scenarios, whether communicating with customers, regulators, suppliers, colleagues, or management/leadership teams. As a Lucid Leader, be sure to model this behavior yourself!
- **Act in good faith.** When dealing with customers, suppliers, and contractors, organizations with high integrity carry out contracts as written and for the benefit of both parties. This applies to internal teams and relationships as well.
- **Be consistent.** Organizations and leaders operating with a high level of integrity address issues from an accepted and unbiased viewpoint. To ensure that rules and guidelines are applied consistently and fairly across the business, they intentionally avoid conflicts of interest and address biases in decision-making.
- **Operate the business as a meritocracy.** Leaders in high-integrity organizations understand that ineffectual employees ultimately hurt the business, and that corrupt behaviors such as cronyism and discrimination rob honest employees of earned opportunities.
- **Meet commitments and obligations.** Organizations and leaders with a high level of integrity do what is required to demonstrate their commitment to effective partnerships and hold up their end of every bargain. They recognize and honor their obligations to customers, employees, regulators, suppliers, and society as a whole.
- **Embrace accountability.** In high-integrity organizations, instead of attempting to pass the buck or blame someone else, individuals take full ownership for their actions. When something fails or goes wrong, they ask themselves, "What could I have done to achieve a better result?"

Keep Integrity Alive

Integrity is not a static or dead thing. It's living and needs to be evaluated and tested regularly.

How can you do this? With these three critical steps.

Step 1: Define Your Values

If you don't know what you truly believe in, you can't live by your values! Start by defining your core values that, no matter what the consequence, you're not going to compromise on.

Some values, like honesty and fair play, should never change. Others might change as you move through life. For example, early in your career, you might have valued learning, flexibility, or achievement. As you advance, you might start to value collaboration, teaching, or stability.

When you're facing challenging conditions in your life, your job, or your organization, your core values help you make the right decisions.

Those people of the cynical persuasion might say, "Hey, it's nice to have integrity, but the market doesn't care. Performance is rewarded, not touchy-feely ethics."

Research studies show otherwise. Finance professor Brandon Cline at Mississippi State University and his coauthors Ralph Walkling and Adam Yore wanted to know if the stock market punished companies for the public transgressions of their leaders. After analyzing data from more than 300 cases of personal indiscretions committed by CEOs of companies between 1978 and 2012 and lining them up against the companies' market performances, they found that personal transgressions were associated with an immediate market decline of 4 percent on average. That might not sound like much, but these were big companies, and the hits averaged $200 million. Over the long run, these firms experienced decline in value of 10 to15 percent.

As NPR's Shankar Vedantam commented, "Once you are identified as a cheater, you always become a cheater."[1]

Step 2: Analyze Your Choices

Often, when people think no one is watching, they cut corners or make self-serving choices. Being integrous means that even when no one is watching, you make the right choice for the greatest number of people.

Yes, many choices we make are morally ambiguous. Let's say you have the opportunity to market a new medical product that will tell people how long they can expect to live. Is this a good thing or a bad thing for people to know? The decision will be difficult, but it must be made by a Lucid Leader who's not compromised by factors such as money or personal ego.

Honesty and integrity are values you should live by all the time, not only when it's convenient. This includes the big choices and the little ones, and the choices everyone sees and those that no one sees.

In 2015, the board of Cabot Creamery, the acclaimed but struggling Vermont dairy producer and cheesemaker, appointed Ed Townley as CEO. He was promoted to the position as much for his personal reputation as his professional competence, as Cabot's board had stated that honesty and integrity were the top two criteria in their search for a new leader.

Soon after Townley moved into his new office, an internal investigation discovered that two managers had been stealing from the company. Townley could have just fired them and swept it under the carpet, thereby keeping the ugly story out of the press. Instead, he had them both criminally charged. They were found guilty and sentenced to prison. He told *Forbes* magazine, "What message would I have sent if I had done otherwise? People needed to know that I was serious about shaping our culture of integrity. It wasn't an easy decision at all, but I knew it was the right one."[2]

Due in no small part to Townley's direction, Cabot became a Certified B-Corp and one of the most respected cheese and dairy brands in the country, able to charge premium prices for its high quality products.

Step 3: Own Your Actions

For the word "integrity" to mean "whole and unbroken," you need to define your values, analyze your choices based on those values, and then take 100 percent ownership of all the decisions you make and everything you do.

This includes when things go wrong.

Especially when things go wrong—even if you are blameless.

The standard of modern industrial integrity was set in 1982, when seven people in Chicago died from consuming Tylenol capsules laced with potassium cyanide. They had all bought the product off the shelf in retail stores. After the story broke, other contaminated bottles were discovered in stores in the Chicago area.

The CEO of Johnson & Johnson, James E. Burke, was widely admired for spearheading the company's decisive, transparent, and generous response. The company swiftly removed all of its products from stores, halted advertising, and assisted law enforcement. It offered to exchange all existing Tylenol capsules for Tylenol tablets, a switch totaling more than 22 million bottles of the capsules in consumers' medicine chests and on pharmacists' shelves worth $80 million at retail prices.

The *Washington Post* said, "Johnson & Johnson has effectively demonstrated how a major business ought to handle a disaster. . . . The company [has not] yielded to the temptation to pillory the media, not even when sensation-seekers tried to link a suicide in Philadelphia in April to the murders in Chicago last week. Not even the publicity-grabbing Chicago prosecutor—who just happens to be running for higher office—has been able to prompt a backlash from the company.

"What J&J executives have done is communicate the message that the company is candid, contrite, and compassionate, committed to solving the murders and protecting the public."[3]

At the time of the tragedy, the company's market share plummeted from 35 percent to 8 percent. In November of 1982, J&J reintroduced Tylenol capsules in a new, triple-sealed package, coupled with heavy price promotions. Within several years, Tylenol had regained the highest market share for the over-the-counter analgesic in America.

Take Action!

- ✓ As a Lucid Leader, you need to *choose* to have integrity in everything you do.
- ✓ There is no test for personal integrity. There's no qualifying exam or certification. It comes from within you.
- ✓ If you choose to cast away your integrity and operate like an outlaw, serving only yourself, you'll probably be able to get away with it for the short term. But such people always get tripped up.
- ✓ The ability to see clearly—to be lucid—does not automatically bring with it a moral component. You must choose to use your powers of clarity and insight with integrity and for the common good, because it's the right thing to do for yourself, your employees, your customers, and your community.
- ✓ In business, integrity begins with you, the Lucid Leader, and needs to be present and robust in every area of the organization. To achieve business integrity, you must:
  - Be honest.
  - Act in good faith.
  - Be consistent.
  - Operate the business as a meritocracy.
  - Meet commitments and obligations.
  - Embrace accountability.
- ✓ Integrity is a living thing and needs to be evaluated and tested regularly. The steps are:
  Step 1: Define Your Values
  Step 2: Analyze Your Choices
  Step 3: Own Your Actions

Lucid Leader Attribute #2: Mission Centered

We have seen that when the Lucid Leader is integrous, the mind is unclouded by internal bias and decision risk can be weighed objectively. There is never a thought of subterfuge or deception. Honesty and transparency are paramount. The relevant information—whether it's reliable or unreliable—is fairly considered.

Integrous is the first attribute of Lucid Leadership. Without it, nothing else is possible.

The second attribute is *mission centered*.

If being integrous describes *how you're going to conduct yourself* while interacting with the external world, your mission describes *the change you seek to make in the world*. In other words, given a set of facts and a decision to make, your choice should support your mission.

You'll notice that I didn't say that your mission is your "destination" or your "goal." While these are the common definitions, neither is precisely accurate. If you say your mission is your destination or goal, you are implying that someday you will arrive there.

And if you should arrive there, then what?

In reality, your mission describes the effect you want to have on the world, or more narrowly, on your market. Because this is an ethical book, we're going to assume that the influence you want to have is positive. You want to make the world a better place. You want to help people solve their problems and be happy. You want your customers to feel better, live longer, enjoy life more.

Most organizations have a mission statement. This book is not about how to write a mission statement. But one example illustrates what I'm saying. One of the most famous corporate mission statements has been used by Wal-Mart for as long as anyone can remember. It's this: "Save people money so they can live better." Two simple phrases.

The first one, "save people money," describes their business model: offer everyday products at the lowest prices possible. Since 1962, that's exactly what they've been doing. You can debate some of their ethics, but in 2022—sixty years later—Wal-Mart was America's biggest corporation by revenue. (Amazon was number 2.)

But you could ask, "What's the point of saving people money? Why is that a desirable outcome?"

The second phrase gives it meaning. The desirable outcome is, "so they can live better." Ah-ha! By saving money, they'll have more money to spend on other stuff, like little luxuries that they might not otherwise have been able to afford. With each dollar, they'll be able to buy more things they want. They'll live more comfortably.

Wal-Mart isn't saying, "We have a product that will make your life better, and you should buy it." Wal-Mart isn't a manufacturer or technology developer. They sell stuff made by other people. Their mission is to make the process you have to go through every day—buying the things you need to maintain your life—slightly less expensive than a competing retailer. By saving you pennies at a time, that extra pocket change quickly adds up.

Solving the Customer's Problem

Assuming the Lucid Leader is not a con artist like Bernie Madoff and seeks to have a positive influence in the world, how does he or she formulate the mission of the company?

Let's imagine that Sally is a recent college graduate armed with a degree in business. Sally wants to be an entrepreneur and start her own company. She wants to work in the B2C space and sell products or services to customers. (Many of the principles we're going to discuss apply just as well to the B2B space, but to keep it simple we'll stick with B2C.) Sally is a smart woman and she could do just about anything.

How should she decide on how she and her company want to affect a change in the world? And more specifically, what can she offer to people for which they will pay money? The more *value* she can offer, the more money people will pay her.

She begins by sitting at her desk with a blank sheet of paper in front of her.

Then she draws two circles. They intersect in what is commonly known as a Venn diagram.

One circle she labels, "What I love do."

The other circle she labels, "What people need and want."

The first circle is relatively easy to populate with activities that Sally could be passionate about. Her passions could include real estate, or finance, or self-care, or pets, or inventing. The key is that they don't have to be super-specific, and the more flexibility Sally has, the more freedom of choice she'll have. But she needs to be passionate about *something*. Being an entrepreneur or the leader of an established business is more than a full-time job, and you need to love it and throw yourself whole-heartedly into it.

For example, when Jeff Bezos decided to quit his high-paying Wall Street job and start his crazy internet book business, he didn't have any particular interest in books. They were just a commodity—something he thought people would buy from a website on the internet. He certainly had no particular fondness for packing those books into cardboard mailers in his garage at night. *His personal mission was not to pack books and haul them to the post office.* That was just the means to the end.

What was he truly passionate about? *He was passionate about inventing a new kind of retail store.* One that had no physical presence, that operated out of a remote warehouse with a website. So if he had made a Venn diagram, in one circle, under "What I love to do," he could have written, "Innovate a new business retail model using the internet." On the other circle, under "What people need and want," he could have written, "A faster and more convenient way to buy books."

He had his mission. At the intersection of those two circles he could have written, "Amazon.com."

Your personal passion—your "why," to use that clumsy and hackneyed term—need not be as grandiose as Bezo's was. You and your company can focus on a problem that seems small. This is what Sara Blakely did. She saw a small problem—the unpleasant sensation of having your feet encased in traditional pantyhose—and set out to solve it. When she began her journey she was hardly an expert in hosiery; her background was in selling fax machines. To get started, she simply cut the feet off a regular pair of pantyhose. Pretty simple! It took some more tinkering to make the idea work, but Blakely was a good salesperson, and she built this little idea into Spanx, a billion-dollar company; and because of her Lucid Leadership she's on the list of America's top self-made female billionaires.

You Need to Be Honest with Yourself

The long-running TV show *Shark Tank* puts entrepreneurs together with investors (the Sharks), in the hopes that the entrepreneur, who is most often also an inventor, will grab the attention of one or more of the Sharks and entice them into making an investment.

Often, a happy marriage is the result. According to *Investopedia*, as of July 2022 the most successful product to have been featured on *Shark Tank* is Bombas, a company that sells comfort socks and T-shirts, and which donates one item per item sold to help the homeless. With $200,000 in funding for a 17.5 percent stake, Daymond John, founder of apparel company FUBU, invested in the company, which generated more than $225 million in lifetime sales. Admittedly, Bombas is not an innovation in the sense that their socks are no different from anyone else's; the innovation is in their charitable business model. But their success indicates that they are filling a need or a want in the marketplace—namely, the need for consumers to *feel good* about the products they buy. We'll explore this theme in much greater depth in the next chapter.

Following Bombas is an invention in the truest sense. Scrub Daddy is a reusable household sponge in the shape of a smiley face. The secret is a patented sponge-like material called FlexTexture that gets firm in cold water and soft in warm water, and has also been lab-tested to rinse clear of debris and resist odors for up to two weeks. Shark Lori Greiner put up $200,000 for a 20 percent stake, and the company has earned $209 million in sales. Clearly, in households across America there was a need for a better kitchen sponge![1]

Inventor Aaron Krause was passionate about his Scrub Daddy product, and after it sat neglected in his garage for five years he brought it out and became convinced it would be a top-selling item. He was right, and the product took off. But being passionate about your invention or new business is no guarantee that it will succeed. You also need to be lucid and able to coldly and objectively assess the value of your product in the marketplace.

For every product that finds an investor on *Shark Tank*, there are many that don't. (The actual figures are unknown because not only are entrepreneurs rejected on the show, but the on-air deals are not legally binding, and roughly half fall apart before the contracts are signed.) The reasons for rejection are many, but one of the most common is that the entrepreneur is passionate about a product that none of the Sharks believe the market wants. Time and time again, a non-lucid inventor claims his gizmo will sell like hotcakes, and the Sharks say, "No it won't. Nobody will buy it."

Sadly, many such entrepreneurs pour their hearts, time, and money into ideas that may seem important to them, or they've talked themselves into believing should be important, but simply aren't. This is the cardinal rule of innovation:

Just because something is *new* doesn't make it *valuable*.

The world is full of new ideas that have no value in the marketplace. The Lucid Leader will be able to objectively assess the facts—including what other people say about the question at hand—and render a decision. Sometimes, that decision means saying, "No."

Yes, Everyone Can Be Wrong Except You!

Having noted that many new ideas are exciting to the inventor but not to anyone else, is it possible that as a Lucid Leader, your vision is *better* than that of most other people, including investors? Are you able to see value where the experts don't?

Yes, it can happen. In fact, it *will* happen. Every innovation gets rejected by someone.

For example, can all five Sharks be wrong about a new product?

Yes.

The most famous example of a massive Shark blunder is the digital doorbell service, Ring. It began in 2013 when inventor Jamie Siminoff appeared on the show to pitch the DoorBot, a doorbell with an integrated video camera that sent alerts and a real-time video feed directly to the owner's smartphone. All of the Sharks declined except Kevin O'Leary, who made an offer that Siminoff thought was unacceptable. He left with no deal.

"I remember after that *Shark Tank* episode literally being in tears," Siminoff told *CNBC Make It*. "I needed the money. We were out of money at the time. . . . I can't count the number of people who didn't invest in this, who said 'no,' the number of people who said it was going to fail."

But other investors did step in, including Sir Richard Branson. Siminoff persisted, and in February 2018, Amazon bought the company—now rebranded as Ring—for more than $1 billion.

In an email statement to CNBC, Ring's spokesperson said in part, "We look forward to being a part of the Amazon team as we work toward our vision for safer neighborhoods."

Note that last phrase: "Our vision for safer neighborhoods." Ring is not in the doorbell business. Their mission is not just to make better doorbells. Their mission is to *create safer neighborhoods.* This is borne out by the fact that when Siminoff was building the first DoorBot prototype in his garage, he was trying to solve a simple problem: When he was working in his garage, he couldn't hear the doorbell. As he told CNBC, he remembered thinking, "I need this damn thing so I can be in my garage inventing." But then his wife remarked that she felt safer having a device that showed you who was at your door. When Siminoff began to envision a bigger mission around home security, he realized he'd found his calling.[2]

What's the lesson here? There are several.

1. Most company missions begin as a tiny seed of something the founder needs or wants but can't get. Blakely wanted more comfortable pantyhose. Siminoff wanted a device that could show you who was at your door. Steve Jobs and Steve Wozniak wanted a user-friendly household computer. Larry Page and Sergey Brin wanted to index the internet. Iris Shamus wanted to keep her child safe from his peanut allergy, so she invented AllerMates, a colorful bracelet for him to wear. There are countless more examples of successful businesses built around a mission of solving a problem faced by the inventor, and the inventor had the skills to succeed.

2. Sometimes what the founder thinks is an amazing innovation that deserves investment and will take the market by storm simply isn't. It's not amazing, or it solves no problem, or it's too expensive, or it's entering an already glutted market. (The last one is Shark Kevin O'Leary's favorite line. He'll say something like, "You are nothing more than a little cockroach who will get crushed in the marketplace." Ouch!)

3. Disruptive innovations always meet some resistance. In 1985, Erik Sandberg-Diment wrote in the *New York Times*: "The portable computer is a dream machine for the few. The limitations come from what people actually do with computers, as opposed to what the marketers expect them to do. On the whole, people don't want to lug a computer with them to the beach or on a train to while away hours they would rather spend reading the sports or business section of the newspaper. Somehow, the microcomputer industry has assumed that everyone would love to have a keyboard grafted on as an extension of their fingers. It just is not so. . . . Because no matter how inexpensive the machines become, and no matter how sophisticated their software, I still can't imagine the average user taking one along when going fishing."[3]

Fast-forward just 20 years. Let's talk about fishing. Do you want a microcomputer to assist you when angling in your favorite fishing hole? Look no further than a product like the ANGLR Bullseye, a device the size of a half-dollar that syncs to the ANGLR app on your smartphone. As you're fishing, just click the Bullseye and it automatically records catch locations, editable waypoints, conditions, and more. It's all uploaded to the GPS-enabled map of your location. At the end of the day, you'll have all your fishing information in as little or as much detail as you need.[4]

Another popular fishing app is Fishbrain. With the app, based on 14 million verified public catch locations, you can learn exactly where your fellow anglers are catching fish and plan your days on the water. It can help you discover new locations and select your fishing spot based on what species you're looking to target.[5]

When Profit Alone Was the Mission

While products and services have always been required to meet a need in the marketplace—that fundamental fact will never change—during the past fifty years companies have evolved in how they view their missions in terms of their relationships to their investors.

The idea that the sole mission of an investor-held company was to deliver profits to its shareholders—called "shareholder primacy"—burst into public consciousness on September 13, 1970, with the publication in the *New York Times* of the article by economist Milton Friedman entitled, "A Friedman Doctrine: The Social Responsibility of Business Is to Increase Its Profits." He bitterly denounced the idea that corporations should use any of their profits—or shareholder money—for anything other than paying back their investors. They should certainly not use any resources—and therefore profits—to pursue a mission that included any form of social activism that did not pay back a monetary return.

Claiming to be exceptionally lucid regarding this topic, he began his article with a direct broadside at corporate social responsibility:

> When I hear businessmen speak eloquently about the "social responsibilities of business in a free-enterprise system," I am reminded of the wonderful line about the Frenchman who discovered at, the age of 70 that he had been speaking prose all his life. The businessmen believe that they are defending free enterprise when they declaim that business is not concerned "merely" with profit but also with promoting desirable "social" ends; that business has a "social conscience" and takes seriously its responsibilities for providing employment, eliminating discrimination, avoiding pollution and whatever else may be the catchwords of the contemporary crop of reformers. In fact they are—or would be if they or anyone else took them seriously—preaching pure and unadulterated socialism. Businessmen who talk this way are unwitting puppets of the intellectual forces that have been undermining the basis of a free society these past decades.

Friedman saw the same set of facts as everyone else, but came to a different conclusion about them. He insisted that the exclusive owners of a business were its shareowners. Everyone else connected with the business was an employee, including the CEO, even if he or she was the founder. The managers of the business were therefore handling other people's money, and were obliged to not waste it on frivolous "feel-good" activities that did not produce an immediate cash return on investment.

Friedman's argument found favor on Wall Street, at least for a few decades. The Friedman Doctrine and similar theories were incredibly influential, and have been credited with ushering in an obsession with quarterly profits, hostile takeovers, colossal frauds, and savage job cuts. In popular culture, the mania reached its peak with the 1987 film *Wall Street*, directed by Oliver Stone and starring Michael Douglas as the unforgettable Gordon Gekko. A corporate raider who cares only about making profitable deals, he doesn't worry about annoying things like ethics. In the most memorable scene, he accused the managers of the Teldar Paper Company of not working to enhance shareholder value, and in a speech that could have been penned by Friedman, said:

> The point is, ladies and gentleman, that greed—for lack of a better word—is good. Greed is right. Greed works. Greed clarifies, cuts through, and captures the essence of the evolutionary spirit. Greed, in all of its forms—greed for life, for money, for love, knowledge—has marked the upward surge of mankind. And greed—you mark my words—will not only save Teldar Paper, but that other malfunctioning corporation called the USA.[6]

But the closer that intelligent, moral people looked at the Friedman Doctrine, the muddier and less lucid it became. Here's a simple example. If an investor were presented with the choice between putting her money into a polluting, abusive diamond mining operation that provided a 6 percent return and a socially responsible company that provided a 5.5 percent return, according to Friedman, the only rational choice would be to invest in the polluting, abusive diamond mine. Hey, it's more profitable right? But the polluting diamond mine creates *significant social and environmental costs that cannot be ignored*. You cannot ignore a toxic river or choking smog, or the medical costs incurred by abusing your workers.

If the company cannot make the appropriate remediating investment from its profits, then who is forced to pick up the bill? The taxpayers do. They must become silent, unrewarded *donors*—not investors—into the polluting diamond mine.

Taxpayers are also compulsory donors to corporations in the case of low wages paid by Wal-Mart and other entry-level employers, whose employees, to survive even when working full time, must turn to public assistance including food stamps, Medicaid, and subsidized housing. The taxpayers are in effect paying a part of the employees' wages.

The Lucid Leader who analyzes the Friedman Doctrine will quickly see that the notion that cash investors are the sole owners of a business may be legally correct, but in reality it's nonsense. The *ideas and labor* of the founders and their employees are a vital part of any business. To succeed, a business needs more than cash. It needs a vision, innovation, and dedication. It also needs support from the government. (Who invented and maintains the assets used by businesses including the internet, and highways, and bridges? Not Milton Friedman!)

Today's Lucid Leader sees clearly the vital role played by investor-owned businesses in our capitalist system, while also appreciating the fact that all businesses exist in a wider community and cannot be separated from it. While it's appropriate that the mission of a company has a narrow focus on the change the organization seeks to make, the very best companies correctly see themselves as part of a human society in which the contribution of every stakeholder is recognized.

The Lucid Leader makes business decisions informed by his or her personal and organizational integrity and by having a clear mission for the company, to which he or she is oriented the way a magnetic needle always points north. The mission of the organization cannot simply be "to make a profit," because that describes every company and does *not* describe the change or improvement the company seeks to make in the community. The mission must saturate the company, reaching into every cubicle and workstation so that it becomes second nature to every stakeholder.

Take Action!

- ✓ The mission of the organization describes an action to be taken to effect a desirable change in the world. In its simplest form, it's, "We do _____ (an action) to _____ (make a change)."
- ✓ The mission must be clearly written so anyone can understand it. While it can be supported by a vision statement and other text elements, the mission statement itself needs to be simple.
- ✓ While the mission statement is a long-range document whose lifespan should be measured in years, it's not set in stone. It should be revisited as necessary to adapt it to industry disruption and changing times.
- ✓ The Lucid Leader embraces the company's mission statement, and strives to ensure that every activity of the company's employees is in alignment with it.
- ✓ There can be a moral or ethical component to the mission. If so, it too should inform the decisions made by the Lucid Leader.

Lucid Leader Attribute #3: Humanistic

We know the Lucid Leader must have personal integrity and a dedication to truth and fair play. He or she must keep themselves and their organization focused squarely on fulfilling their mission to make a beneficial change in the world by solving a problem for the customer. These values should be on display every day and in every way.

The third attribute of the Lucid Leader is *humanistic*.

This means the Lucid Leader needs to be oriented toward humanism. For our purposes, this means having an outlook or system of thought attaching prime importance to an organization's human assets rather than regarding people as just another cost center. Humanist beliefs emphasize common human needs, stress the potential value and goodness of human beings, and seek fair-minded ways of solving human problems.

The inclusion of humanistic as the third attribute is necessary because every company engages in a wide range of activities. It sells a product or service at a profit. (This keeps Mr. Friedman happy.) It provides jobs for people in the community. (We have yet to see a company that requires no employees.) It influences the overall cultural fabric of the community, hopefully in a positive way by raising the quality of life. It supports other businesses in the B2B space, such as suppliers and media outlets. It can even provide charitable services that would otherwise be the responsibility of the government, and for which it's compensated with the appropriate tax deduction.

For its success, every company depends on having a close working relationship between the leaders and the employees. Whether the number of employees is one hundred or one hundred thousand, they all must function as a cohesive unit with a common sense of integrity and focus on the mission.

It's the job of the Lucid Leader to make this happen, and to make the organization's employees as productive as possible.

But how? Specifically, how does the leader inspire, cajole, beg, threaten, or otherwise motivate his or her employees to excel?

Just like technology has accelerated its pace of disruption, the conventional wisdom of how to treat employees to maximize their productivity continues to rapidly evolve.

The Bad Old Days

In the nineteenth century, as the factory system blossomed, workers were treated like a commodity. Conditions in city factories were harsh and led to deadly accidents. The workday was commonly twelve hours. Tasks tended to be divided purely for the sake of industrial efficiency, which led to repetitive and monotonous work for employees. Because of the ready supply of unskilled labor streaming off the farms and into the cities, if a worker got injured or fed up and quit, they'd quickly be replaced. Many workers were provided with company housing, and then charged so much for it they had not a penny left at the end of the month.

Here's the testimony of Ann Eggley, age 18, who worked in an English coal mine in 1842: "I'm sure I don't know how to spell my name. We go at four in the morning, and sometimes at half-past four. We begin to work as soon as we get down. We get out after four, sometimes at five, in the evening. We work the whole time except an hour for dinner, and sometimes we haven't time to eat."

And her sister, Elizabeth, age 16: "I hurry in the same pit, and work for my father. I find my work very much too hard for me. I hurry alone. It tries me in my arms and back most. We go to work between four and five in the morning. If we are not there by half past five we are not allowed to go down at all. We come out at four, five, or six at night as it happens. We stop in generally 12 hours, and sometimes longer."[1]

Now that's a relentless pursuit of profit above all else!

The philosophy held by the owners was that workers were nothing more than illiterate laborers, not much better than cattle. To make them more productive you simply made them work longer hours. Any question about their "happiness" was absurd and irrelevant.

The Better New Days

Fast-forward nearly two centuries, and much has changed in the industrialized nations. (Sadly, some emerging economies of Southeast Asia and Africa look more like 1842.) Today, we do little non-farm labor that's purely manual. Even automobile assembly line work requires more brains than brawn. Because the human brain becomes fatigued before the muscles do, you cannot get more productivity by forcing your employees to work longer hours in poor conditions. In fact, studies have shown that working *fewer* hours in *pleasant* conditions *increases* productivity while *lowering* liability costs.

In America, we're working fewer hours than our ancestors. In 1840, the average workweek was 68 hours. By 1900 it had fallen to 58 hours. In 1926, Henry Ford—the nation's largest employer—adopted the five-day workweek. By 1960, the average industrial workweek was down to 41 hours, and 1988, 39 hours.[2]

But working conditions still matter, and they aren't always ideal. Many companies are "pressure cookers," where employees are driven hard. As *Harvard Business Review* noted, the American Psychological Association estimates that each year workplace stress drains more than $500 billion from the American economy and 550 million workdays are lost due to stress on the job. Health care expenditures at high-pressure companies are nearly 50 percent greater than at other organizations. Workplace stress has been linked to health problems ranging from metabolic syndrome to cardiovascular disease and mortality. As much as 80 percent of workplace accidents are attributed to stress, and more than 80 percent of doctor visits are due to stress.

Authors Emma Seppälä and Kim Cameron add that stress-producing bosses are literally bad for the heart: In a large-scale study of over 3,000 employees conducted by Anna Nyberg at the Karolinska Institute, results showed a strong link between leadership behavior and heart disease in employees.[3]

Accelerated by the Covid-19 pandemic and the corresponding Great Resignation, we're living in an age of radical transformation in the workplace. People are working fewer hours and demanding greater flexibility and less stress. Schedules like all-remote or hybrid, which before the pandemic were completely unthinkable for most people, are now becoming part of work mainstream. The idea of shortening the workweek is also gaining traction, spurred by workforces that have successfully trialed a workweek with reduced hours.

A shorter workweek could take various forms. There's the four-day week, reducing your working hours by 20 percent. There are various scheduling models; at one company everyone might take the same day off, or if you need a constant presence of someone in the office or the store, doing it in rotation.

The Value of Employee Happiness

Regardless of the number of hours people work, researchers are discovering that the level of *employee happiness* is critical to organizational success.

Happiness? Isn't that some kind of touchy-feely, "give-every-kid-a-trophy" kind of sentiment?

Okay—let's ask the U.S. Army. If any organization should be oblivious to employee happiness, it's the Army, right?

Wrong.

Researchers Paul B. Lester, Ed Diener, and Martin Seligman followed nearly one million U.S. Army service members for five years, measuring their relative happiness and optimism using 25 questions drawn from PANAS and the Life Orientation Test. The questions were included on a larger survey taken by every Army soldier each year.

As reported by *MIT Sloan Management Review*, this well-being measurement combined the soldiers' self-assessments and reporting on the frequency of positive and negative emotions experienced, to yield a measurement of happiness.

Even after the researchers controlled for a range of demographic factors and previous performance, soldiers who said they were happy and optimistic went on to earn significantly more job performance awards across the next five years compared with those who were initially unhappy and pessimistic.[4]

Among civilian workers, research by Oxford University's Saïd Business School, in collaboration with British multinational telecoms firm BT, found a conclusive link between happiness and productivity.

Their study into happiness and productivity, conducted in the call centers of BT over a six-month period in 2019, revealed that workers are 13 percent more productive when happy.

"We found that when workers are happier, they work faster by making more calls per hour worked and, importantly, convert more calls to sales," noted Professor Jan-Emmanuel De Neve, one of the study's authors.[5]

Ever hear the expression "happy warrior"? It's from a poem by William Wordsworth. This is the person, as Wordsworth says, "Whose high endeavours are an inward light, that makes the path before him always bright."

Whether in the army or in your company, you need the happy warrior. The opposite of the happy warrior is the "sad sack," a non-lucid type who sees nothing but negativity, doom, and gloom. If you have such a person on your payroll, either reform them or get rid of them as quickly as possible.

The Humanistic Workplace

Employee happiness is just one facet of what we call *the humanistic workplace.*

The humanistic workplace emphasizes the whole person and the uniqueness of each individual. It begins with the existential assumptions that people have free will and are motivated to achieve their potential and self-actualize. It spotlights the personal worth of the individual, the centrality of human values, and the creative, active nature of human beings. It's fundamentally optimistic and highlights the noble human capacity to overcome hardship, pain, and despair. Each person, in his or her own, seeks to grow psychologically and continuously enhance themselves.

In psychology, the humanistic principles are these:

1. The most significant aspect of a person is their present functioning. The "here and now" matters far more than examining the past or attempting to predict the future.
2. Whether their actions are positive or negative, mentally healthy individuals take personal responsibility for them.
3. Simply by existing, each person is inherently worthy. While a given action may be negative, it does not cancel out the value of a person.
4. The ultimate goal of living is to attain personal growth and understanding. Only through constant self-improvement and self-understanding can an individual ever be truly happy.

The Lucid Leader embraces these principles, not only for themselves but as a framework for their relationship with employees and all stakeholders.

The concept of humanism is closely related to the Hierarchy of Needs presented by Abraham Maslow in his 1943 paper "A Theory of Human Motivation" in the journal *Psychological Review*. This hierarchy is a foundation for understanding *task motivation*—that is to say, an employee's self-generated desire to willingly perform their job. All people are motivated by a succession of needs, from the most basic survival needs to the highest spiritual needs.

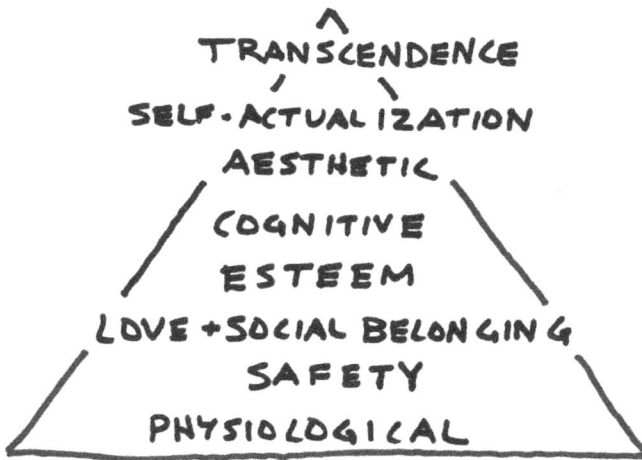

Originally there were seven, and later Maslow added the eighth. They are:

1. **Physiological needs.** These are the requirements for biological survival: food, air, water, shelter.
2. **Safety needs.** To not just survive but thrive, humans need physical, emotional, and financial stability and security. They need not just one paycheck, but a *steady* paycheck.
3. **Love and social belonging needs.** Humans are social animals, and will go to great lengths to feel as though they belong to a group or family.
4. **Esteem needs.** Maslow noted two versions of esteem. The "lower" version is the need for respect from others. The "higher"

version is the need for self-respect and can include a need for self-confidence, competence, independence, strength, mastery, and freedom.

5. **Cognitive needs.** Humans have the most powerful brains of any species, and we're happiest when we can use them! We have curiosity and a will to learn and attain knowledge. This is the first level that is unattainable by most animals.

6. **Aesthetic needs.** This is a continuation of cognitive needs, and represents the ability and desire to appreciate the beauty of the external world, as well as a desire to appear beautiful to others.

7. **Self-actualization.** This was originally the highest level, and summed up by the quote, "What a man can be, he must be." (Women too, of course!) Humans are naturally motivated to pursue goals in life—to become a doctor or lawyer, succeed in business, write a book, or have a family.

8. **Transcendence needs.** Most people find their fullest satisfaction in giving themselves to something beyond themselves—for example, in altruism or spirituality. Maslow equated this with the desire to reach the infinite and become connected with the wider universe through science, philanthropy, spirituality, or art.

What does this have to do with the Lucid Leader?

Plenty.

In the context of the workplace, Maslow linked task motivation to unmet needs at any level. If an employee has unmet needs and no hope of meeting those needs, he or she will become disengaged and will slow down and achieve less. This could happen at any stage, although in our highly developed industrial society with social welfare safety nets, most employers will be able to satisfy levels 1 and 2—physiological and safety needs. I said "most" employers because sadly there are many that pay employees less than a living wage, and many of these people are stuck at level 2, trying to maintain their sense of financial security.

Only when lower-level needs including physiological and safety needs are met can workers successfully move up the hierarchy and—with the support of the Lucid Leader—eventually self-actualize, becoming highly motivated workers.

Lucid Employees—the Leaders of Tomorrow

This book is focused on the leader of the organization and what he or she needs to accomplish, and within these pages we discuss the importance of being a Lucid Leader.

Our focus on the leader is mostly a matter of expediency, because in many ways there should be no difference between the Lucid Leader and his or her employees. Everyone in the organization, from the loading dock to the boardroom, should have personal integrity. Every person should be focused on the mission and be humanistic. Every person should be lucid and see reality clearly, even when they see danger and disruption.

In addition to making the organization work in the present, everyone—especially the CEO and the board of directors—needs to look ahead into the future and see new opportunities and obstacles. This is being lucid at its very best! And one of the most important things to consider about the future is organizational leadership. You need to ask, "In five, ten, or twenty years, who will be working in the corner office? Where will this person come from? Will we be able to find future Lucid Leaders from within our own ranks?"

Right now, there could be a future CEO within your ranks. Someone like Mary Barra, who spent 34 years as an employee of General Motors before taking the helm in 2014. Or Planet Fitness CEO Chris Rondeau, who 20 years earlier had started as a front desk receptionist at his neighborhood location. Or Michael Corbat, who fresh out of college in 1983 joined the sales department at Salomon Brothers, which subsequently merged with Citigroup, where he was named CEO in 2012.

Barra, Rondeau, and Corbat didn't become overnight Lucid Leaders when they took the reins of their respective companies. They each had been a Lucid Employee for many years, seeing their environment clearly, making sound decisions, and moving their departments ahead.

How many Lucid Employees do you have in your organization right now who could climb the ladder and assume greater responsibility?

Self-Care

You've been on a commercial airliner during the pre-flight safety lecture by the flight attendant when he or she talks about what to do if the oxygen mask drops from its overhead compartment. If you're traveling with a small child, you must first put a mask on your own face. Only then should you place a mask on your child. You first, then your child.

Why? *Because you must ensure your own ability to act.* If for some reason you didn't do that, and there was a delay in putting a mask on your squirming child, then you might lose consciousness, and both you and your child would be in great danger.

As the Lucid Leader—both on the plane and in your corner office—you need to practice self-care, and be ready to respond when the need arises.

You cannot run yourself ragged solving every little problem. You need to delegate and build a team of Lucid Employees who can meet challenges on their own. This is not because you're lazy or want to escape to the golf course every Friday. It's because you're looking for maximum *efficiency* and *leverage*.

"Efficiency" means no wasted time. It means no redundancy—that is, fixing the same problem twice. It means delivering maximum value to your customers and your investors.

"Leverage" means making the most of your time and skills. For example, which would be better for a CEO: to spend an hour talking to the facilities manager about the problem of employee trash in the break room, or spending an hour talking to the CEO of a company in Europe about a possible joint venture? As the Lucid Leader, you need to do only those jobs that *no one else can do.*

Make it a company rule: At the end of the day, everyone goes home (or if they're working remotely, logs off). No after-hours email. Mandatory vacations. And make these rules apply to yourself as well!

Benefit Corporations

In the previous chapter we discussed the Friedman Doctrine, which asserted that the only non-debatable duty of the CEO was to deliver profits to the investors. In the decades since, his view has fallen into disfavor, and today, even those companies that remain relentlessly profit-driven try to appear as though they have embraced social and environmental responsibility.

The Lucid Leader knows that attitudes of investors, employees, and customers have changed. There is wide acceptance of corporate social and environmental responsibility, which means acting as a responsible steward of the communities they serve.

To make such a humanistic commitment public and verifiable, companies have two choices, similar but different.

- **Benefit corporation.** In the United States, where it's authorized by 35 U.S. states and the District of Columbia, a benefit corporation is a form of for-profit corporate entity whose stated mission includes having a positive impact on society, workers, the community, and the environment. In addition to earning a profit for its investors, the definition of "best interest of the corporation" is specified to include those impacts.

  Such a designation has been deemed necessary because the charters of conventional corporations (referred to as "C corporations" by the IRS) do not clearly define what is meant by "best interest of the corporation." This opens the board of directors to attack by Friedman-esque shareholders who demand that increasing shareholder value is the *sole* overarching or compelling interest of a corporation.

Designating the organization as a benefit corporation insulates boards from such attacks and allows the company to be socially responsible.

- **B-Corporation.** This is an earned certification from B Lab, a nonprofit organization that's spearheading the drive toward a new, stakeholder-driven business model. The B Lab organization certifies B Corporations, which are companies that meet the organization's standards of social and environmental performance, accountability, and transparency. When making business decisions, certified B Corporations are legally required to consider the impact of those decisions on all of their stakeholders—a model known as *stakeholder governance*. The B Corp legal framework allows companies to protect their mission and ensures that the company will continue to practice stakeholder governance even after capital raises, leadership changes, and even when evaluating potential sale and liquidity options.

The movement is growing. As of May 2022, the B Corp community included 5,000 B Corps companies with over 400,000 workers in 154 industries across 79 countries.

Take Action!

✓ The Lucid Leader needs to be keenly aware of trends in employment. The Covid-19 pandemic sent shock waves through many industries, and the management assumptions leaders held pre-pandemic may no longer be valid. Keep your ear to the ground!

✓ Employee happiness is important for your bottom line. You need to be looking for "happy warriors" who support the organization's mission and want to go the extra mile for your customers. If you have "sad sacks," you need to either reform them or get rid of them ASAP.

✓ The humanistic workplace emphasizes the personal worth of the individual, the centrality of human values, and the creative, active nature of human beings. That needs to be your goal.

✓ In their daily work, all people are motivated by a succession of needs, identical to those espoused by Abraham Maslow. Only when lower-level needs are met can workers successfully move up the hierarchy. Ensure that your organization can satisfy all of those needs and be home to highly motivated workers.

✓ One of the most important things to consider about the future is organizational leadership. You need to ensure your organization has people who could climb the ladder and assume greater responsibility.

✓ As the Lucid Leader, you need to practice self-care and be ready to respond when the need arises. Delegate and, when you go home, do not check your email!

✓ Today's corporations are expected to act like good citizens while they turn a profit. If you haven't already, investigate becoming a benefit corporation or a certified B-Corp, or both. Investors are increasingly showing a preference for companies based on a humanistic foundation.

Lucid Leader Attribute #4: Innovative

After being integrous, mission-centered, and humanistic, the fourth attribute of a Lucid Leader is to be innovative.

What do we mean by "innovative?"

In business, to be innovative means that you *create novel value that serves your organization and customers.*

Let's look at the three key words in our definition:

1. **Create.** In the case of the Lucid Leader, this could mean that you personally are an inventor of new processes, products, or technologies, like Bill Gates or Sara Blakely. But it's more likely that through your leadership of your organization, you support and develop the efforts of creative people on your team, like Jeff Bezos or Sir Richard Branson support theirs.

2. **Novel.** Put simply, this is something new to the market. It either presents a new way of solving an old problem or it solves a new problem.

3. **Value.** What you create and sell to people must have value to them. It must be useful or desirable. If it has no value, no one will want to pay for it, and your company will go bankrupt.

There have been many books written about organizational innovation, including several of my own. This book and this chapter are focused on *you,* the person, who as the leader must be innovative as a personal quality. If you do not have an affinity for innovation, then you cannot hope to lead an organization for which innovation is necessary for survival.

Throughout history, while individual humans have always shown a penchant for innovation, the *rate* of innovation has been accelerating to the extent that we regularly experience not just incremental change to our lives but *sudden disruptions*. Innovations that once took decades to filter through our lives now take just a few months or even weeks. Leaders who could plod along year after year with few changes in their perception of the world are now buffeted by bold new ideas.

The Lucid Leader needs to see these trends clearly. He or she cannot ignore accelerating disruption. It won't be going away. It's here to stay. Instead, the Lucid Leader must wholeheartedly *embrace* disruptive innovation and leverage it to his or her advantage.

Here's the aphorism that every Lucid Leader must take to heart:

When it happens to you, disruption is your enemy.
When you're the cause of it, disruption is your friend.

If you're a business owner and suddenly a competitor offers a new product that's better than yours and at a lower price, that's disruption that you don't want. It's happening to you and could even put you out of business.

But if you're the disruptor, and you're innovating and staying ahead of the competition, then disruption is good for you.

As a leader, would you rather be on the receiving end of disruption or the one dishing it out?

Do you want to be a typical leader who's always a step behind, or a *disruptive leader* who forges ahead boldly, laying the course for others to follow, and staying ahead?

You may ask, "How can any Lucid Leader keep ahead of the relentless pace of disruption? Aren't there too many new ideas constantly flooding into the market?"

Relax—the Lucid Leader doesn't need to understand the endless minutia of every little emerging technology, consumer behavior, or economic shift. He or she does not need to personally be an inventor, but someone who supports the people who are.

Imagine an old-fashioned circus. You, the Lucid Leader, are the ringmaster. You stand in the center and direct the show. You are *not* a lion tamer. You are *not* a tightrope walker or a juggler. You need not be able to do these things—they are in the domains of trained professionals. Your job is to keep the show running smoothly and ensure the seats are filled with paying customers.

Above all, Lucid Leaders are brave and show a willingness to lean into their own executive development by driving the changes occurring both within their organization and outside in the markets and economies they serve.

Innovation Does Not Always Mean a Shiny New Invention

Many leaders are afraid of innovation because they think the only things that qualify as innovative are new physical inventions that you can get patented. They think of innovators as people like Steve Jobs who introduce amazing new products to the market. These are things that the press writes about and consumers rave about on social media.

This definition makes many excellent leaders nervous. They say, "My business isn't going to change the world. I'm not Steve Jobs or Sara Blakely." Or, "We're a service business. We don't make new products." Or, "Our product is ubiquitous. We're not high-tech."

To this we say, "Relax. Most innovations are not shiny new inventions. They appear behind the scenes, in processes and ways of thinking, in supply chains and marketing campaigns. While most businesses aren't going to be massive market disruptors, *any* business can innovate and stay ahead of their competition."

There are functional areas in your business ready for innovation. As a Lucid Leader, all you have to do is identify them and nurture them.

There's even a word for it: *hidden innovation*.

Originally coined in the 1990s by Diana Hicks and Sylvan Katz in their research on the hidden biomedical research systems involving hospital researchers, and Mike Hopkins's research on genetic testing within the UK healthcare system, the concept of hidden innovation became more widely known through the UK nonprofit Nesta in their 2006 report *The Innovation Gap*. A later report, *Hidden Innovation*, further expanded on the concept and identified four types of hidden innovation:

1. Innovation that is the same or similar to activities that are measured by traditional indicators, but which is excluded from measurement.
2. Innovation without a major scientific/technological basis, such as innovation in organizational forms or business models.
3. Innovation created from the novel combination of existing technologies and processes.
4. Locally developed, small-scale innovations that take place "under the radar" and are therefore unrecognized or accounted for.[1]

The point of this is that you, the Lucid Leader, need not *personally* be an inventor or innovator. But you must know how to hire, encourage, and fund people who are innovators, and then put their new ideas to work in a way that ultimately benefits your customers, investors, and the broader community.

Reality Cannot Be Invented

Today's innovation leaders know the first step toward leveraging disruption is to recognize the world *as it really is* and not *as they'd like it to be*.

They know that many things can be invented—but reality is not one of them.

Successful leaders chase *truth*, not *assumptions*.

Leaders achieve success only *after* they've been honest and truthful about what's required to drive enterprise excellence. Any effort built on a misguided perception of reality is bound to fail.

This applies to how you manage your teams. You need to be honest about what you're asking them to do, and then you need to address the realities of the challenges head-on. Disruption requires that you recognize what's really happening and respond decisively, without thinking, "We can't do that!"

It applies to how you view your competitors.

To *overestimate* them is dangerous because it may cause you to back away from an opportunity that could be successful for you. When Martin Eberhard and Marc Tarpenning founded Tesla Motors in 2003 (Elon Musk didn't invest until the following year), they didn't think, "Are we crazy? How can we compete against Toyota, VW, GM, and the other global automakers?" Instead, they saw an opening in the market into which they could insert themselves and grow.

To *underestimate* your competitors is equally dangerous and perhaps more common. The history books are full of big companies that underestimated a disruptive threat and were eventually crushed by it. Perhaps the most famous example is Blockbuster Video, which in the year 2000 brushed off the opportunity to buy Netflix. Ten years later, Blockbuster declared bankruptcy. In 2021, the upstart Netflix, having become a global entertainment producer and distributor, posted $29.7 billion in revenues.

Having established the value of innovation and the imperative that you and your company must drive disruption rather than be victimized by it, the next question you may ask is, "How do I, being a regular, non-genius person, develop my powers of innovation?"

You can do it. You don't need to be a rocket scientist or a software genius. You can learn the skill of innovation just like any other. You just have to follow these steps and stay focused on the eternal truth that *the only constant is change.*

Get Organized!

The Lucid Leader is not intimidated by the complexity of innovation.

This is a good thing, because the world is becoming increasingly byzantine, and there are many leaders who respond to it by doing one of two things:

1. They try to ignore it. They throw up their hands and say, "Oh, let's just keep doing things the way we've always done them!"
2. Or they seek to master every aspect of some new technology or system, and wind up in a hopeless tangle, paralyzed with indecision. Others look to such leaders for guidance, and the leaders reply, "Wait. We need another piece of information." And another, and then another. This is analysis paralysis, and it can be a fatal affliction.

The key to managing the onrushing flood of innovation and all its complexity is to do five things:

1. See it clearly. Not every detail, but the general contours.
2. Quickly sort out the innovations that are possibly useful versus the ones that are not useful.
3. Develop the innovations that show promise. If necessary, invest in them. You want to embrace innovations that provide *new value to your customers.*

4. Deploy the ones that are going to bring new value to your customers.
5. Track their performance, if possible. Review their return on investment.

Does this process look familiar?

It should. It resembles a traditional sales funnel, which scoops up all the possible leads and puts them through a process of filtration. As the leads pass through the funnel and its various filters, the worthless prospects drop out while the potential sales keep moving ahead.

It also resembles the innovation pipeline that I introduced in my best-selling book *The Innovation Mandate*.

Just like your organization has a sales pipeline, it needs an innovation pipeline. It's no different than a sales pipeline, just that it's full of new ideas rather than new sales. Your innovation pipeline needs to be overseen by you and managed by your employees. Unless your company is a real startup with just you and a partner working out of your garage, you'll need dedicated sales and marketing people on the innovation pipeline. Your job is to keep it organized and profitable.

So much for your *company*. Because you're a leader, you also need to informally keep an innovation pipeline *in your head* or in a notebook. Read voraciously and keep an eye out for news items about emerging technologies. Make mental or physical notes about whether an emerging technology can help you conquer new markets or revitalize a moribund brand. Set aside some time each day to think creatively and write down any ideas you might have.

You need to be able to imagine the future from a simple concept, as well as envision the steps it will take to achieve a particular goal.

Learn how to apply innovation and creativity to managing people and projects. The ability to apply innovation is especially important in times of uncertainty, ambiguity, and risk, and the Lucid Leader inspires productivity in new ways and through different approaches than have typically been used and taken.

Be ready to consider a novel concept or approach that's challenging for those who cling to the tried and true methods. Innovative leaders can recognize fresh ideas from their team members and work to develop paths and success from those ideas. The Lucid Leader is eager to embrace change, experiment with new concepts, and envision the path forward for a creative idea.

A Lucid Idea Reinvents a Boring Product

Everyone knows Old Spice men's personal care products. The venerable brand was launched in 1937, and by the turn of the century it occupied the space next to carmaker Oldsmobile as the product your dad might use if he were really boring. The parent company, Procter & Gamble, was ready to sell off the moribund brand. In 2006, the company tossed Old Spice to the advertising company of Wieden + Kennedy. See what you can do with this old fossil, said P&G.

The people at Wieden + Kennedy saw reality: The product was as good as any other, but it needed a bold and innovative marketing approach. So they hired actor and former NFL wide receiver Isaiah Mustafa. The guy is a hunk! For the first ad in the series, they put him in a towel next to a shower, and with a cheeky grin he addressed the women viewers: "Hello, ladies. Look at your man. Now back to me. Now back to your man. Now back to me. Sadly, he isn't me. But if he stopped using ladies' scented bodywash and used Old Spice, he could smell like he was me." The scene cut to a yacht in the Caribbean, then suddenly Mustafa was astride a white stallion. The 30-second mini-movie ended with the familiar Old Spice whistle.[2]

The ad was an immediate sensation. After going viral online, it won the Grand Prix at Cannes, inarguably the most prestigious advertising award. During mid-2010, the series of "Smell Like a Man, Man" spots held 8 of the top 11 most-popular videos on YouTube.

The ad was written by Craig Allen and Eric Kallman of Wieden + Kennedy. They set aside all the preconceptions and cultural baggage surrounding Old Spice and asked, "What's the clear answer? How can we make young men—and women—look at this product with fresh eyes?"

The answer: "We'll make it fun, sexy, and irreverent. In that order."

It's all about clearly *seeing* the associations that have developed around a product, *choosing* whether to keep or discard them, and then boldly *acting* to create a new set of associations.

Take Action!

- ✓ To be innovative means that you *create novel value that serves your organization and customers.*
- ✓ Remember the aphorism that every Lucid Leader must take to heart: *When it happens to you, disruption is your enemy. When you're the cause of it, disruption is your friend.*
- ✓ Hidden innovation is important! This includes innovation in organizational forms or business models, innovation created from the novel combination of existing technologies and processes, and locally developed, small-scale innovations that take place "under the radar" and are therefore unrecognized or accounted for.
- ✓ Lucid Leaders chase *truth*, not *assumptions*.

✓ The key to managing the onrushing flood of innovation and all its complexity is to do five things:
1. See it clearly.
2. Quickly identify the innovations that may be useful.
3. Develop the innovations that show promise.
4. Deploy the ones that are going to bring new value to your customers.
5. Track their performance.

✓ You need to be able to imagine the future from a simple concept, and then envision the steps it will take to achieve a particular goal.

✓ Learn from the successful Old Spice reboot: Innovation can mean taking a familiar, shopworn product and marketing it in a new, fresh way.

Expanding the
Knowledge Horizon

This chapter is about the *knowledge horizon* held by humans and particularly leaders.

This refers to the limits of knowledge attainable by leaders in the execution of their daily responsibilities. Those limits are expanding at an increasingly faster rate.

If you think about it, for thousands of years, a leader had three ways of knowing what was going on in their organization, such as an empire, an army battalion, a religious group, or a feudal estate. These three ways were very simple.

1. Direct personal observation of an event. This was uncommon, because no leader can be everywhere at one time. The leader's range of knowledge was literally the visible horizon.

2. A report of an event delivered orally by a trusted person. This was most common—every leader had a network of subordinates

and spies. This capability extended the leader's range of knowledge over the visible horizon.

3. A written communication, such as a letter. This was fairly common, but letters took time to physically deliver. In theory, with written letters, the range of knowledge could extend around the world.

The problem was that *the greater the distance the knowledge traveled, the older it became.* If an event happened in the same room as you, then you saw it in real time. But news of an event that happened fifty miles away might be two days old, and news of an event that happened 5,000 miles away would be months or even years old. Your response to the news would take an equal amount of time to travel to its destination far over the horizon.

For example, consider the Dutch East India Company. Chartered in 1602, it's considered the first modern global corporation, with business interests in Eurasia (mainly in Greater India and the Asia-Pacific region) and southern Africa. In the seventeenth century, the sailing time from Amsterdam to the Dutch East Indies was six months. With a few weeks' turnaround time before the return trip, a ship could easily be gone—and out of communication with—the home office for well over a year. If it was wrecked along the way, years might pass before critical business information filtered back to Amsterdam.

Or how about this: on January 1, 1863, President Abraham Lincoln issued the Emancipation Proclamation, freeing enslaved people in the United States. News of the proclamation began to travel throughout the nation. But it was not until over two years later, on June 19, 1865, with the announcement by Union Army general Gordon Granger in Galveston, Texas, that the news finally reached every corner of the nation.

Leaping ahead to the late twentieth century, business leaders had the telephone (with "long distance" calls abroad) and the newfangled fax machine, which could transmit documents over physical phone lines.

With accelerating technology, the twenty-first century brought instant digital communications, both voice and print, followed by video services including Skype, which was supplanted by Zoom.

For information processing, computers became ubiquitous. They allowed leaders to take large quantities of *known data* and quickly process it to find patterns and trends. For example, DNA analysis requires vast amounts of storage space and processing speed, both of which emerged in the first decade of the twenty-first century, making sequencing fast and affordable.

These advances allowed leaders to become more lucid in regard to their ability to get information about events and developments occurring at a distance, as well as complex events happening anywhere.

Artificial Intelligence

By the third decade of the century, artificial intelligence (AI) was beginning to emerge as a potent tool to expand the knowledge horizon of leaders.

Artificial intelligence is loosely defined as systems or machines that mimic human intelligence to perform tasks and can iteratively improve themselves based on the information they collect. It's become a catch-all term for applications that perform complex tasks that once required human input, such as playing chess or communicating with customers online. Although AI brings up images of high-functioning, human-like robots taking over the world, it isn't intended to replace humans. It's intended to significantly enhance human capabilities and contributions. That makes it a very valuable business asset.

Artificial intelligence is often used interchangeably with terms including "machine learning" and "deep learning." But there are differences. For example, machine learning is focused on building systems that learn or improve their performance based on the data they consume. But while all machine learning is AI, not all AI is machine learning.

In general, AI systems learn to recognize patterns in data in much the same way as the human brain learns. If you show a child 1,000 pictures of varieties of apples, the child will learn to recognize the characteristics of an apple. Then if you show a child a picture of a lemon, despite some general commonalities with an apple, the child will be able to say, "That's not an apple. It's something different."

In this case, the pictures of the apples are what AI scientists call *labeled training data*.

By ingesting large amounts of labeled training data and analyzing the data for correlations and patterns, the AI-capable computer can make predictions about future states. For example, an image recognition tool can learn to identify and describe objects in images by reviewing millions of examples. Those objects could be tiny cancerous growths in human tissue.

A chatbot that is fed examples of text chats and rules of grammar can learn to produce lifelike audio exchanges with people.

These processes are made possible by *algorithms*. An algorithm is a set of rules to be followed in calculations or other problem-solving operations. The goal of an algorithm is to produce an answer by following a sequence of steps. For instance, in everyday life, a recipe used to make a cake is an algorithm.

An algorithm tells a computer what to do next with an "and," "or," or "not" statement. Such as, "1 and 1 equals _____" Obviously, like most things related to mathematics, it starts off very simple, but when expanded, becomes infinitely complex!

A research study by Infosys that polled over 1,000 global C-level executives at large organizations across seven markets revealed that AI is becoming a core aspect of business strategy. Broad adoption of AI is impacting every aspect of the way leaders do their jobs, including the way they drive innovation and compete, inspire teams, recruit and train, and apply AI and human power together to achieve their vision for the company. Forty-five percent of IT decision makers report improved process performance from AI and 40 percent report productivity gains due to IT time spent on higher-value innovative work.

A primary factor driving ROI from AI was the presence of a clearly defined strategy. Eighty percent of respondents who said they've seen at least some measurable benefits from AI also noted their organization had a defined strategy for deploying AI.

Lucid Leaders have to evolve quickly in a disruptive and dynamic environment, and to bridge the gap between old and new business and work realities they need to champion change throughout the organization.

Seventy-six percent of all respondents were either confident or extremely confident that the senior leaders of their organization understand and promote the positive aspects of AI.[1]

A Computer on the Board of Directors?

In 2014, A Hong Kong VC fund announced it had appointed a computer to its board, with voting power.

Strictly speaking, Deep Knowledge Ventures, a firm that focuses on age-related disease drugs and regenerative medicine projects, claimed to have appointed an algorithm called VITAL, which could make investment recommendations about life sciences firms by analyzing large amounts of data.

"[The goal] is actually to draw attention developing it as an independent decision maker," Deep Knowledge Venture's Charles Groome told *Business Insider.*[2]

Dmitry Kaminskiy, managing partner of DKV, said that the fund would have gone under without VITAL because it would have invested in "overhyped projects." VITAL, which stands for Validating Investment

Tool for Advancing Life Sciences, helped the board make more logical decisions, he said.[3]

Speaking of "overhyped," when the announcement received widespread press coverage, industry professionals responded with a healthy dose of skepticism. Michael Osborne, an associate professor in machine learning at the University of Oxford, said, "Essentially, all I think they're doing is using the predictions made by this algorithm as kind of a starting point for discussion on the board, which I think is a totally reasonable thing to do, but I think it's a bit of a gimmick to call that an actual board member."[4]

Another small detail is that according to Hong Kong law, board members must be actual human beings.

But the point was made: AI is increasingly being used to expand the knowledge horizon of Lucid Leaders, giving them insights that are deep and can be produced quickly. More effectively than the human mind? Legendary investor Warren Buffett might have a thing or two to say about that. But not every human being is Warren Buffett.

This leads to an interesting point. Humans have very complex skill sets. In terms of evolution, some of those skills have been a part of our operating systems for millions of years, such as facial and voice recognition, navigating through space, catching a ball, judging people's motivations, setting future goals, and all the skills that we use for attention, visualization, perception, movement, socializing. These are "easy" skills that we can do without conscious thought.

In addition, we possess skills that we've developed in more recent times: mathematics, engineering, scientific reasoning. These require conscious thought. They do not come easily to us—they are the "hard" skills.

As it turns out, AI algorithms are good at these "hard" skills and not so good at the older, "easy" skills.

This has led to what is called Moravec's paradox. Articulated by robotics and computer scientists Hans Moravec, Rodney Brooks, Marvin Minsky, and others in the 1980s, it's the observation that, contrary to traditional assumptions, reasoning requires very little computational resources, but sensorimotor and perception skills require enormous amounts. As Moravec wrote in 1988, "It is comparatively easy to make computers exhibit adult level performance on intelligence tests or playing checkers, and difficult or impossible to give them the skills of a one-year-old when it comes to perception and mobility."[5]

In the development of AI, computer scientists were initially successful at writing programs that used logic; played complex games, including checkers and chess; and solved algebra and geometry problems. These tasks are difficult for most people and are considered a sign of intelligence. Many researchers assumed that having made progress solving the problems that were "hard" for humans, the "easy" problems of vision and common-sense reasoning would soon follow. They were mistaken. Such problems are extremely difficult to solve, but we humans, with millions of years of practice, make them appear easy.

In business, we must make do with the skills and capabilities we possess while seeking help with the tasks that are more difficult—and for many Lucid Leaders, an AI algorithm can provide that extra competitive edge.

Worker Productivity Tracking

Disruptive innovation is a double-edged sword. New technology brings new benefits and new challenges. It can make life easier and more productive while raising ethical and even legal questions.

Worker productivity has always been subject to measurement. Since the earliest days of the Industrial Revolution, assembly line employees have been judged by how many widgets they can produce in a day. In a manufacturing plant, everyone works out in the open, within plain view of managers. If you fail to keep up or make your quota, you're fired or demoted to pushing a broom.

Salespeople are judged by their productivity. Clerks are rated by how many files they process. CEOs are judged by the company's stock price. These are metrics that are easy to see and measure.

Unlike the assembly and clerical workers of yesteryear, today's white-collar office employee is often not under the direct supervision of a manager. He or she is increasingly located away from the office, delivering digital work products from a remote location. Other employees work in their traditional cubicles, but toiling out of sight of a supervisor, while some work a few days at home and a few days in the office. Hybrid work gives employees more freedom to conduct their business day on their own schedule, which many see as a significant benefit.

This hybrid work model creates challenges for managers, particularly when it comes to understanding their employees' productivity. They lack the insights they would gather when employees worked openly and delivered measurable product. They can't see if their employee—whether remote or on premises—is focused on the company project or watching cat videos on YouTube. He or she may even be using the company computer to send out their resume to apply for a job elsewhere.

The advent of digital technology has given employers powerful new tools for collecting data on the daily interactions of employees with the tools they use to do their jobs. The amount and type of data that can be collected is astonishing, right down to the last keystroke or restroom break.

Snoopware Is Big Business

These new technologies fall under the moniker *snoopware*, also known as *bossware* or *spyware*. They offer employers a range of features including keystroke logging, screenshots of workers' computers, and even access to webcams.

For example, Teramind offers a suite of digital tools that track and quantify employee behavior. According to the Miami, Florida-based company, the feature called "in-app field parsing" collects granular terminal and web app activity metrics that reveal how employees utilize and navigate individual fields and field level data. "Screen capture" allows managers to use the computer's built-in camera to see employee actions in real time or in the past. "Remote desktop control" permits the boss to take remote control over an employee's computer, or disable the keyboard and mouse during a monitored session. Managers can see desktop file activity including creation, deletion, access, writing, and transfer operations. They can monitor employee email activity and record keyboard activity including copy+paste commands and visible or invisible keyboard entries.[6]

Another company, Veriato, offers its AI-powered Cerebral security platform as a tool to "detect threats from employees" by "proactively recognizing signs of risk, like changes in an employee's attitude and behavioral patterns," thereby allowing managers to take action. The Cerebral algorithm alerts the manager to an employee exhibiting signs of disengagement, such as agitation or the use of profanity or selected keywords, and shows related screen shots so that the manager can determine the true nature of the incident, and collect the evidence essential to taking legal action.

The West Palm Beach, Florida, company also provides the now-ubiquitous snoopware services of keystroke logging, network monitoring, file tracking, chat activity, and even psycholinguistic analysis, which identifies and categorizes opinions expressed in email texts, revealing if the employee has become "disgruntled" and a possible security risk.[7]

Based in Austin, Texas, ActivTrak says it takes a more employee-friendly, "ethical" approach that claims to boost productivity without the use of intrusive employee monitoring technologies like keystroke logging and video surveillance. Nevertheless, the company uses the same basic snoopware tools that have become common to monitor employees, including assessing the total time an employee spends on productive and unproductive activities, revealing when employees are actively working or taking breaks throughout the day, and analyzing productivity for individuals or teams throughout the day.[8]

Companies like Activtrak are careful to reassure employees and managers that Big Brother isn't looming over their shoulders. They present the surveillance as a tool for increased team productivity and a way to help team members become more productive. If used properly, such tools could be an asset to a responsible company.

In low-level jobs, monitoring has become ubiquitous. Amazon is the poster child, where the second-by-second measurements are notorious. But it's being used to oversee UPS drivers, Kroger cashiers, and millions of others. According to an examination by the *New York Times*, 8 of the 10 largest private U.S. employers track the productivity metrics of individual workers, many in real time.

Digital productivity monitoring is become commonplace among roles that require graduate degrees and white-collar workers. An increasing number of employees, whether working in the office or remotely, are subject to a variety of snoopware trackers, productivity scores, "idle" buttons that need to be minded, or just the drip-drip of constantly accumulating records. Gaps in one's active work record can incur penalties, from docked pay to lost jobs.

At companies, including J.P. Morgan, tracking how employees spend their time, from composing emails to making phone calls to, has become routine practice. At UnitedHealth Group, low keyboard activity can affect compensation and sap bonuses. Some radiologists see scoreboards displaying their "inactivity" time and how their productivity compares to that of their colleagues. Government jobs can be tracked, too: in June 2022, New York's Metropolitan Transportation Authority told engineers and other employees they could work remotely one day a week if they agreed to full-time productivity monitoring.

Tracking can now be applied to the physiology of the employee. Microsoft holds a patent titled "Emotion Detection from Contextual Signals for Surfacing Wellness Insights." The software giant describes a "wellness insights service" that amasses biometric data from a range of wearable devices, including fitness trackers, digital assistants, and smartwatches.

Blood pressure and heart rate monitoring data obtained from wearables can assess an employee's stress levels during routine work tasks, including drafting and reading emails and attending meetings. If the employee registers elevated anxiety or stress, the wellness insight service may trigger an intervention related to the work event.[9]

The non-Lucid Leader might hear about this technology and immediately think, "This is terrific! It's just what I need to get my lazy employees to work harder! No shirking at my company—no sirree! Where do I sign up?"

To that we say, "Not so fast."

Snoopware comes with two significant liabilities that employers need to appreciate.

It's Often Inaccurate

Across industries and incomes, the most urgent complaint is that snoopware is often just wrong. It misses productive offline activity, it's unreliable at assessing hard-to-quantify tasks and prone to undermining the work itself.

Reports are common of social workers being marked "idle" for lack of keyboard activity while counseling patients in drug treatment facilities. Solving a difficult problem for a customer sometimes takes time that cannot be tracked. Working out a human resources issue may not count. And trying a new idea—an innovation—that ultimately doesn't work could be perceived as wasted time.

In "The Rise of the Worker Productivity Score," Jodi Kantor and Arya Sundaram tell the story of a finance manager named Carol Kraemer. She was not a file clerk or a call center customer service rep—the kind of lower-level employee you might assume would be subject to productivity tracking. She was a senior vice president, earning $200 an hour while she worked remotely.

When she received her first paychecks, the amounts seemed low. What was the problem? Some clerical error in human resources? No. The problem was that her new employer used extensive monitoring software on its all-remote workers. She and others were paid only for the minutes when the system detected what it considered to be *active work*. That meant when Carol was doing something that was visible and measurable, like typing on her computer.

In Carol's opinion, the software did not come close to capturing all of her labor. Any "offline" work, such as reading printouts, doing math problems on a calculator, or just thinking about a problem, didn't register and required approval as "manual time." In managing the organization's finances, Carol regularly interacted with a dozen people, but those interactions didn't always register with the algorithm. If she forgot to turn on her manual time tracker, she had to make a special request and explain what she was doing that warranted being paid.

She said sometimes she resorted to doing mindless busywork to accumulate clicks.

"You're supposed to be a trusted member of your team, but there was never any trust that you were working for the team," she said.[10]

It's Demeaning

Let's face it: it's one thing to work in an open office, surrounded by colleagues who can generally see what you're doing and will know if you're sitting at your desk playing Candy Crush Saga instead of working. It's something else entirely to feel as though Big Brother were tracking your every keystroke and every trip to the restroom, and will dock your pay for every measured infraction.

In general, in the United States, the laws and the courts favor the employer. While the U.S. Constitution contains no express right to privacy, the U.S. Supreme Court has historically upheld an implied right to privacy at home, but *not to employees*. Courts favor the idea that since the company owns the equipment and the office space, it has a right to monitor its employees to prevent misuse of that equipment and space. Even if workers use their personal devices at home, their employer could still legally track their activity if they're using company email accounts, networks, or servers.

While employers are required to inform employees that they retain the right to monitor their behavior, but these notices can be vague and found buried in the fine print of the employee's contract or company handbook. There's no requirement for employers to tell workers specifically what monitoring programs they're using or what sort of information they are gathering.

Here's the basic rule: if the employer *owns* it, the employer can *monitor* it.

In many companies with particularly heavy-handed surveillance programs, employees are resisting. Office workers are echoing complaints that lower-paid employees have voiced for years: they say they don't have control and their jobs are relentless, without even a spare few minutes to use the restroom.

In 2019, Barclays bank piloted a software system called Sapience, which, according to the vendor's website, gave companies "insights into work patterns" and tracked productivity by monitoring employees' computer use. The bank would even send intrusive and condescending messages to workers such as, "Not enough time in the Zone yesterday." In February of 2020, after negative staff feedback and critical media reports, the bank backtracked and announced that moving forward, the software would collect only anonymized data.[11]

As Camilla Winlo, director of data privacy consultancy DQM GRC, said, "The problem isn't the monitoring itself, but the fact that the intrusion into employees' privacy doesn't match the scale of the threat. Although most detective controls—those used to identify risks—will require some trade-off between workers' privacy and their safety, such tools can result in monitoring not just employees' work habits, but their overall lifestyle choices . . . workers may also be legitimately using a computer in a private capacity from their own home."[12]

Commander's Intent

This is the bottom line: Who are you hiring? And how are you training them?

The foundation of Lucid Leadership is that you create a culture of trust in your organization, and you hire people who will fit into that culture. You train them to embrace trust and expect it every day. If you cannot trust someone to do their job, don't hire them.

Here's a powerful example. In the U.S. Marine Corps, trust between all Marines, regardless of rank, is paramount. This foundation of trust is expressed in a concept known as "commander's intent." This means that the individual Marines who are told to complete a mission are provided with a set of instructions, which they are *empowered to abandon if conditions on the ground require it*. For example, if a captain says to a rifle team, "Your mission is to take and hold that hill. You will attack the hill from the south." But if the rifle team gets to the target and sees the south side is impassable, while the north side presents an opportunity, the leader has the authority to say, "We're going to attack from the north."

It's the responsibility of the leader of the rifle team to be lucid, to see the problem, and to execute the commander's intent, which is to capture and hold the hill.

In such situations, trust and lucidity are mandatory.

Distrust is inherently an expression of a false reality. By this we mean that you hire a person, you train them, and you give them responsibility. You say to them, "These are the goals we need to reach. We will give you the tools—the computer, the phone, the office—to reach those goals. You are empowered to use your best judgment. Get the job done!"

So far, so good! But then you say, "Oh, and by the way, *because we don't trust you,* we're going to monitor those tools we provided. Our computer will be watching you and tracking every move you make. Have a nice day—and be loyal to the company that loves you!"

Sounds crazy, right? But that's exactly what non-lucid companies are saying to their employees. They think that they can treat their employees like prison inmates, and then those employees will reciprocate with loyalty and hard work.

Fat chance.

To be fair, let's consider the opposing viewpoint. We can hear CEOs saying, "How are we supposed to know if our employee is goofing off while on our payroll? The employee is working at home, out of sight. We need these surveillance tools!"

Go back to the commander's intent. You solve the problem very simply. You say to the employee, "Your goal is to complete this report/project/chart/draft by tomorrow/next week/every month. Can you do that? Yes? Good. We will leave you alone to get it done."

You can say this to the employee regardless of their physical location. They could be working at home, in a satellite office you own, or in the cubicle down the hall from you. It doesn't matter. You give them the job and they do it.

The opposing viewpoint might reply, "But wait! Isn't the title of this book *The Lucid Leader*? I'm trying to be super-lucid and know everything that's going on with my employees. The more information I have about their activities, the better!"

If your employee were a machine, we'd agree. We *need* performance data from machines. Take our automobiles. It's amazing that every new car has a full suite of computer diagnostics to alert the owner of the slightest problem. Do you have a tire that's underinflated? The diagnostics will tell you. Are you drifting out of your lane while driving? The computer will beep you a warning.

But—and we'll only say this once—*people are not machines*. Even assembly line and data entry workers, who perform machine-like tasks, are not machines. The people who pack boxes in Amazon fulfillment centers are not machines, despite Mr. Bezos's dreams to the contrary.

Human beings are driven by emotion as much as by logic. The Lucid Leader needs accurate information about how his or her employees *feel* about their jobs and their lives. The happier the employee, the more dedicated and loyal they will be. To learn all you need to know about happy employees, check out Nick's best-selling book *Happy Work: Why Your Organization Needs to Create a Culture of Happiness*.

The Lucid Leader will take the time and effort required to get to know his or her direct reports (at the very least) and build a culture of trust. This culture must include the most remote people on the lowest rungs of the pay scale. Remember—trusted people work harder and deliver better results!

Take Action!

✓ Advances in AI technology allow leaders to become more lucid in regard to their ability to make decisions. AI algorithms can collect information about complex events, process that information, weigh the choices or solutions, and offer a recommendation—which the human leader is free to accept or reject.

✓ AI is becoming a core aspect of business strategy. The keyword is "strategy." Your organization must develop a plan for how you can leverage AI and how you intend to measure the return on investment. The AI strategy must be connected and coordinated across the enterprise, and in close alignment with the overarching business strategy.

✓ Just because it's AI doesn't mean you should embrace it! Tools are just tools, and they can either be used constructively or misused and cause damage. Be judicious with employee surveillance programs. They don't give you the full picture of the employee's activities, and they can cause a feeling of resentment. Instead, hire your people carefully and focus on developing a culture of trust.

How to Become a Lucid Leader in Four Steps

As with so many things in life, while the goal may be clearly in sight, the question looms: How do I get there? Where do I start? What path do I take?

Here are the four steps. Take them one at a time. Results will not come overnight! It has taken most of us a lifetime to accumulate the mental and spiritual baggage that can weigh us down, prevent us from seeing clearly, and impede decisive action. Getting rid of the baggage can take time.

Step 1: Get Clear

The first step to becoming a Lucid Leader is to get out your mental Windex and clean your windows of the gunk that's preventing you from seeing clearly.

This applies to both the external world that you see through the window and the internal world—yourself—that you see in the mirror.

The ability to see clearly involves knowing the difference between three types of knowledge or thought processes that take up space in your brain. They are:

1. **Legitimate knowledge.** This is what qualifies you to do your job, lets you drive to work every morning, pay your bills on time, and otherwise live your life. It's the career experience that builds from year to year, the academic learning you acquire, and the insights you gain from facing life's many challenges. It's what makes a grandparent self-assured when handling the new baby presented by the nervous son or daughter—Grandma has seen it all before, and it's no problem!

2. **A vision of tomorrow.** This ability is what literally separates us from all other animals. We can imagine the world as a better place and take action to make it a reality. A vision of tomorrow is rooted in the facts we know today and, based on those facts, our uniquely human ability to extrapolate new possibilities.

   It's when an inventor thinks, "I know we have the internet. We have video cameras. These are facts. Why can't we combine the two and create internet videoconferencing systems?" Innovation comes from our ability to perceive a situation as a problem and our desire to correct the problem. Sometimes such innovations are within reach, and other times we know they are out of reach—at least for now.

3. **Misleading assumptions.** While having a vision of the future makes human civilization possible, its evil twin, misleading assumptions, can be a big problem. Misleading assumptions are unverified beliefs that people cling to because they seem to align with their legitimate knowledge, but in fact there's no basis for making such a connection. It's when a leader says, "A person of a particular race or ethnicity or age cannot be a good worker." Or, "I only trust my own judgment. I don't need a bunch of advisors. I don't need to change my way of thinking."

To ensure your mental Windex has done a good job, you need to apply it to both the windows that look outside and the mirror that reflects your own image back at you.

The Windows That Look Outside

Misleading assumptions about the world will interfere with a leader's ability to see clearly. In business they are very common. A particularly egregious example relates to demographics and the persistent belief that people who belong to generational groups (Baby Boomer, Gen X, Millennials, Gen Y, and so forth) can be pigeonholed according to their expectations as consumers. One group is supposedly more lazy, one group is more spiritual, one group more thrifty, and so on. It's true that their interest in specific products and services will vary. A Baby Boomer nearing retirement is more interested in her Social Security benefits than is a 20-year-old member of Gen Z, for whom retirement is a lifetime away. And marketing punk rocker Machine Gun Kelly to the AARP crowd might be a waste of money. But that has nothing to do with their personalities and how they want to be treated as customers or employees. Marketers and employers constantly pigeonhole people by superficial demographic markers, and as a result lose customers and employees by making false assumptions.

An employer might think, "I'm not going to hire a kid with long hair because I'm sure he'll be unreliable," when in fact there's no basis for such a belief and the specific kid in question might be an incredibly hard worker.

As a Lucid Leader, your first task is to make sure you are seeing reality and not relying upon a picture of the world that's based on erroneous data.

When we say "the world," that includes yourself.

The Mirror That Reflects Your Image

We have many preconceptions about ourselves that, in the context of our performance as leaders, can lead us to make poor decisions. Here are just a few mental deceptions we foist upon ourselves.

1. **You doubt yourself.** Your assessment of an opportunity may be clouded by your own doubts about whether you have the skills or ability to manage it. This form of cognitive interference has a negative motivational effect and inhibits your ability to accurately process information.

   Limiting beliefs can be overcome with simple techniques such as identifying people who diminish your self-esteem. If you surround yourself by people who are positive and encourage you, you will have more mental energy to focus on excellence.

2. **You see only obstacles, not the victory.** Researchers note the difference between a *promotion focus* and a *prevention focus*. The former is when you perceive a goal as being reachable despite the challenges that you'll encounter. The latter is when you see the same challenges and, because you have a negative mindset, you conclude the goal is not attainable.

   When there is success feedback and promotion focus framing, the goal will seem closer, and when there is failure feedback and prevention focus framing, the same goal will seem more distant.

3. **You see only victory, not the obstacles.** The opposite problem is self-aggrandizement. Here, you assume that anything you do will be successful. How you got this way is anyone's guess, but it probably came from your parents, who gave you everything you wanted. (The human personality has deep roots in childhood.) In any case, while self-confidence is a good thing, being blind to challenges is foolish. *The world does not owe you a living.* "Get real," as they say, and understand that if you have an idea, it's guaranteed that many other smart people have exactly the same idea. The victory will go to the person who makes the extra effort.

Step 2: Become Overqualified

Becoming clear is the first step. You're an empty vessel, so to speak. Transparent. Able to see clearly in all directions, like a child, for the first time.

The fact is that every human being begins life as a *tabula rasa*—a blank slate. Every corporate leader and business mogul was once a naïve and unschooled child. Somehow they learned. Many learned by doing. Sir Richard Branson attempted to grow and sell Christmas trees and then budgies, or parakeets, and failed. At the age of 16 he launched a magazine named *Student* with Nik Powell. When the magazine began losing money in the late 1960s, he formed Virgin Mail Order Records, named because Branson considered himself inexperienced in business. In 1971 he opened the first British discount record store, and then the record label, Virgin Records, which still exists today.

He's had several notable failures: Virgin Cola, Virgin Cars, Virgin Publishing, Virgin Clothing, and Virgin Brides (the last one was an attempt to enter the lucrative wedding industry). He has said, "I suppose the secret to bouncing back is not only to be unafraid of failures but to use them as motivational and learning tools. . . . There's nothing wrong with making mistakes as long as you don't make the same ones over and over again."[1]

Other leaders have taken a more traditional route and have gotten a formal education. Perhaps the most well-known example is Jeff Bezos, who graduated from Princeton University with degrees in electrical engineering and computer science (not business!). He then went to Wall Street, where he worked at Bankers Trust and D.E. Shaw & Co., a hedge fund. At the age of 30, he left to start Amazon.com. As we saw in Chapter 7, while he knew nothing about packing books, he knew a lot about how to build a business!

Like other people, you possess a lifetime of knowledge. Some of it from school, some from family, some from the streets or the playground. The trick is to make this vast storehouse of knowledge something that *you can control*, not that controls you.

It may seem weird to say that, but it's true. So much of what we think and believe is colored by the past—how we were treated as a kid, our success or lack of success in school, the things our parents or church tried to teach us about the world. These colorations can prod us to interpret information one way or another.

If your school principal tells you that you're stupid and cannot succeed—as Nick's principal told him!—those words will make a difference. They can defeat you or motivate you. They'll certainly stay with you as long as you live!

All of this knowledge—including people's opinions of us—is there, in the mind, ready to be put to constructive use.

The Lucid Leader must build on that knowledge. The reasons are simple: the more you know, the more clearly you see the world. And because of the accelerating rate of change in the world, you need to work to stay ahead of the curve.

Earlier in the book we used the example of a jet fighter pilot. Today's Air Force pilots require months of intensive training and at least 100 hours of flight time to "get a seat" in an aircraft cockpit. When they take the controls of one of today's sophisticated planes, they face an array of instruments that would bewilder a person who wasn't qualified. The average person wouldn't even know where to begin!

Business is no different—with the only exception being that in business you can learn by doing, and if you crash, you're probably not going to die in a fireball. But the business leader sitting in the cockpit of his or her craft sees, and must understand, an array of metrics and tools that to the untrained outsider would be perplexing.

When commanding your business, the more you know about how it works, the more clearly you will see. Ignorance is not bliss, it's misery. Big mistakes are made by leaders who don't know what they don't know, and who make false assumptions. They climb into the cockpit, see the myriad of instruments and toggles and levers, and start fiddling with them, willy-nilly.

By "overqualified," we don't mean that you need to know everything about every aspect of your business. That's impossible, especially as your business grows. But you do need to be able to ask the right questions. You need to know if the answer you get sounds right. If one of your vice presidents says, "We need to do X, Y, and Z," you need to have enough knowledge to make an intelligent and well-informed decision.

As Diogenes said, "Wise leaders generally have wise counselors because it takes a wise person themselves to distinguish them." You need to know enough to distinguish wise counsel from partisan or ill-founded opinions.

Step 3: Embrace Lifelong Learning

Having become overqualified and capable of making informed decisions, does that mean you can now relax and go with the flow?

Sorry! As the old saying goes, there's no rest for the weary.

Whether you do it in an academic setting, with a mentor, or with self-directed study, maintaining a habit of lifelong learning benefits you and your organization in many ways.

- **Help your brain stay healthy.** Recent research has found that learning keeps brain cells working at optimum levels, which may slow cognitive and memory decline as we age. "When you exercise, you engage your muscles to help improve overall health," says Dr. Ipsit Vahia, director of geriatric outpatient services for Harvard-affiliated McLean Hospital. "The same concept applies to the brain. You need to exercise it with new challenges to keep it healthy."[2]

- **Stay connected.** Many types of group continuing education allow you to meet new people and connect with the innovations of today. As a Lucid Leader, to keep making friends and stay in touch with accelerating disruption, one of the best choices you can make is to continue learning.
- **Get a bigger paycheck.** Job promotions go to lucid people who keep up with the latest information and technology. The Pew Research Center found that 87 percent of adults in the workforce agree that it will be essential or important for them to get training and develop new skills throughout their careers to keep up with changes in the workplace.[3]
- **Stay confident.** If a Lucid Leader hasn't stepped out of their routine for a while, taken on a new challenge, or applied themselves to learning something new, they may find the experience intimidating. With lifelong learning, this fear is more easily overcome. It helps the leader maintain their confidence in their ability to learn and to share the information with others.
- **Be more self-fulfilled.** In 2015, Doreetha Daniels received her associate degree in social sciences from College of the Canyons, in Santa Clarita, California. At the time she donned her cap and gown, she was 99 years old. In the COC press release about her graduation, Daniels indicated that she wanted to get her degree simply to better herself. Her six years of study were a testament to her will, determination, and commitment to learning.

Alvin Toffler, the American futurist, writer, and businessperson, said, "The illiterate of the twenty-first century will not be those who cannot read and write, but those who cannot learn, unlearn, and relearn."[5]

While it may have particular urgency today, lifelong learning is not a new idea. In 1562, at the age of 87, the artist Michelangelo expressed the essence of this idea when he inscribed the words "*Ancaro Impari*" ("I'm still learning") on a sketch he was developing.

Some leaders claim they have no time to learn. The fact is that people do what's important to them. Even leaders with many responsibilities can make choices about how they spend their time. We once knew a successful CEO who became convinced that playing golf every weekend was necessary for his emotional health. We have nothing against recreation—as we like to say, "all work and no play leads to mental and spiritual decay"—but really? Every weekend? Sadly, this person's company lost its competitive edge and was eventually bought for a fraction of its former value.

Make learning a priority. If you don't have time to physically go to a class, read books. (Like this one.) Or take a class online. Attend lectures. Or be like Warren Buffett and begin your day by reading. "I still probably spend five or six hours a day reading," Buffett says in HBO's documentary, *Becoming Warren Buffett*. "I like to sit and think. I spend a lot of time doing that and sometimes it is pretty unproductive, but I find it enjoyable to think about business or investment problems." (We bet he's glad his computer doesn't have a keystroke tracker and a boss who demands a quota of keystrokes per hour!) Buffett typically reads six newspapers each day: the *Wall Street Journal,* the *Financial Times,* the *New York Times,* the *USA Today,* the *Omaha World-Herald,* and *American Banker.*

Mark Cuban agrees. He wrote that when he was starting out in business, "Everything I read was public. Anyone could buy the same books and magazines. The same information was available to anyone who wanted it. Most people won't put in the time to get a knowledge advantage." And now, "To this day, I feel like if I put in enough time consuming all the information available, particularly with the internet making it so readily available, I can get an advantage in any technology business."[6]

Step 4: Set Up Systems

We know that being CEO or a top leader is not exactly a walk in the park. Your time is precious. That's why you need to be lucid about how you allocate your hours.

In our work with global CEOs, who are very smart people, we've found an astonishing number of them waste their valuable time in performing tasks that are far below their pay grade.

Here are just a few examples of time wasters—and what you can do to free yourself from them and get lucid!

1. **Emails and low-value interruptions.** This is the rule: you cannot control what your subordinates ask you to do. But you must control how you respond to them.

   You need to set your priorities, make them known, and stick to them. If you don't consciously come into work every day with a plan to do your most important work, answering emails is an easy default. Don't hesitate to use automation tools, including calendaring platforms, to block off uninterrupted focus time. That's the time you should use to build strategic relationships and focus entirely on the future of the company.

   Set clear communications guidelines to empower your teams to do their own work and tackle problems. Answer only those emails that will help a subordinate solve a significant problem. For most of them, simply reply, "I trust you to use your best judgment." And then—this is crucial—back up your words with integrity. If you empower a subordinate to do a job, and they fail—*for whatever reason*—you are just as accountable as they are. You need to focus on solving the problem and getting that person trained to handle the challenges he or she faces.

2. **Pointless meetings.** An effective meeting requires preparation, both from the facilitator and the attendees. A clear agenda and the opportunity to review materials in advance leads to productivity and minimal wasted time.

   Too many meetings devolve into boring marathons full of endless PowerPoint presentations. Managers must not be rewarded for spouting incomprehensible business jargon but for zeroing in on a problem and presenting a solution.

3. **Failure to delegate.** A common danger for leaders and founders is a failure to delegate as the company grows. Assigning routine tasks to others is imperative! As the Lucid Leader, if you are bogged down with minutiae and not focusing on the business, then nobody is driving strategy.

   This is where business systems are important. As the business grows or as new initiatives are added, there must be repeatable systems put into place that will drive down the expense—in time and money—of performing routine tasks.

4. **Too many projects.** The Lucid Leader needs to prioritize, both for his or her own sanity but also for every other employee. It's better to have fewer priorities and try to move one project through. Every time a new initiative crosses your desk, you should ask yourself these three questions:

   • Is this a key driver of value for our business and our customers? Will it add to our bottom line? If the answer is "no," then delegate it down the chain of command. Get it off your desk. If "yes," then ask . . .

   • Does this problem require my personal involvement? If the answer is "no," then delegate. If "yes," then ask . . .

   • At what level do I need to get involved? Should I keep at a high level and oversee others, or personally take charge? Answer the question and respond accordingly.

   • Save the solution and use it again! This is key. No one in your organization should *ever* have to solve the same problem twice. To be required to do so is an extreme waste. Once the problem has been solved for the first time, ensure the solution is memorialized so that when the same problem appears again, the solution can be repeated.

Take Action!

Becoming a Lucid Leader requires four steps. They are:

- ✓ **Step 1: Get clear.** Know the difference between *legitimate knowledge*, having a *vision of tomorrow*, and *misleading assumptions*. You want the first two. Number three is bad. Clear your mind of misleading assumptions and work with reality.

    Be sure to see the outside world clearly, as well as yourself. Self-doubt is just as counterproductive as self-aggrandizement.
- ✓ **Step 2: Become overqualified.** As the Lucid Leader, you need to be able to see the big picture as well as key details. The more you know about how your business works, the more clearly you see. You need not know everything about every aspect of your business, but you do need to be able to ask the right questions and know enough to make an intelligent and well-informed decision.
- ✓ **Step 3: Embrace lifelong learning.** Maintaining a habit of mental exploration benefits you and your organization.
- ✓ **Step 4: Set up systems.** As the Lucid Leader, you need to *see* the critical problems and *decide* how to solve them. Does a problem require your personal attention or can you delegate? And then once the problem has been solved, ensure the solution is accessible so that when the same problem arises again—which it will—the systematic solution is at hand.

Thank You!

Thank you for reading this book. To learn more about how we can help you to become a Lucid Leader and take your organization to the next level, please contact us.

Acknowledgments from Nicholas

I would like to acknowledge all of the hard work and dedication of my coauthor and son, Chase Webb. His fresh and contemporary perspective provided a tremendous multigenerational view of this important subject.

I would also like to thank my colleagues, and the research team at LeaderLogic® and LearnLogic® for helping bring this book to life.

I would also like to thank my clients for allowing me to share some of my direct experience in leadership development, board facilitation, training, and consulting, providing real-world actionable insights to help me bring the theoretical into the practical.

Notes

Chapter 1

1. Bloomberg. https://www.bloomberg.com/graphics/2021-congestion-at-americas-busiest-port-strains-global-supply-chain/.

Chapter 2

1. CNN Money. https://money.cnn.com/2011/08/30/autos/akio_toyoda_toyota.fortune/index.htm.
2. NYT. Zen and the Art of Computing, John Taylor, *The New York Times*, October, 25 1987.
3. https://thehustle.co/How-People-Describe-Working-for-the-Most-Powerful-Leaders-in-the-World/.
4. The Atlantic. https://www.theatlantic.com/business/archive/2011/11/be-a-jerk-the-worst-business-lesson-from-the-steve-jobs-biography/249136/.
5. https://www.linkedin.com/pulse/macho-business-leaders-ray-williams/.

Chapter 3

1. SHRM. https://www.shrm.org/resourcesandtools/hr-topics/compensation/pages/employers-respond-to-resignation-tsunami-by-raising-pay-improving

-benefits.aspx#:~:text=Employers%20are%20responding%20by%20 adjusting,on%20board%2C%20SHRM's%20researchers%20found.

2. https://www.mac-history.net/apple-history-tv/2008-07-19/macworld -boston-1997-steve-jobs-returns-bill-gates-appeares-on-screen.

3. https://www.globenewswire.com/en/news-release/2020/08/28/2085261/ 28124/en/10-Billion-Worldwide-Online-Survey-Software-Industry-to -2025-Retail-is-Widely-Using-Online-Survey-Software-for-Understanding -Consumer-Behavior.html.

4. https://www.prnewswire.com/news-releases/labor-day-survey-51-of-us -employees-overall-satisfied-with-their-job-300704255.html.

5. https://www.payscale.com/research-and-insights/professional-development -employees-want/.

6. SHRM. https://www.shrm.org/hr-today/trends-and-forecasting/research -and-surveys/Documents/2016-Employee-Job-Satisfaction-and-Engagement -Report.pdf.

Chapter 4

1. https://www.teslarati.com/vw-fired-herbert-diess/.

2. Vox.com. https://www.vox.com/culture/2019/12/3/20993432/peloton-new -commercial-horror-movie.

3. NYT. https://www.nytimes.com/2022/08/12/business/peloton-job-cuts -higher-prices.html.

Chapter 5

1. https://www.licenseglobal.com/rankings-and-lists/top-150-leading -licensors-2019.

2. Car and Driver. https://www.caranddriver.com/news/a37187201/ford-build -to-order-online-ordering-changes/.

3. https://skeepers.io/en/blog/how-customer-feedback-surveys-helps-apple -maintains-industry-leadership/.

4. SurveyAnyPlace.com https://surveyanyplace.com/survey-fatigue/.

Chapter 6

1. NPR. https://www.npr.org/2018/07/24/631742105/marks-punish-behavior -that-reflects-a-ceo-s-lack-of-integrity.

2. Forbes. https://www.forbes.com/sites/roncarucci/2021/05/19/to-unify-his -company-around-integrity-this-ceo-sent-people-to-prison/?sh=65782c272e1d.

3. WAPO. https://www.washingtonpost.com/archive/business/1982/10/11/tylenols-maker-shows-how-to-respond-to-crisis/bc8df898-3fcf-443f-bc2f-e6fbd639a5a3/.

Chapter 7

1. https://www.investopedia.com/articles/investing/082415/10-most-successful-products-shark-tank.asp.
2. CNBC. https://www.cnbc.com/2018/02/27/amazon-buys-ring-a-former-shark-tank-reject.html.
3. NYT. https://timesmachine.nytimes.com/timesmachine/1985/12/08/206974.html?pageNumber=278.
4. ANGLR. https://shop.anglr.com/products/anglr-bullseye.
5. Fishbrain. https://fishbrain.com/pro.
6. https://www.americanrhetoric.com/MovieSpeeches/moviespeechwallstreet.html.

Chapter 8

1. https://www.encyclopedia.com/social-sciences/applied-and-social-sciences-magazines/testimony-ann-and-elizabeth-eggley-child-mine-workers.
2. https://eh.net/encyclopedia/hours-of-work-in-u-s-history/.
3. HBR. https://hbr.org/2015/12/proof-that-positive-work-cultures-are-more-productive.
4. MIT Sloan. https://sloanreview.mit.edu/article/top-performers-have-a-superpower-happiness/.
5. Oxford U. https://www.ox.ac.uk/news/2019-10-24-happy-workers-are-13-more-productive.

Chapter 9

1. Nesta.org. https://www.nesta.org.uk/report/hidden-innovation/.
2. https://www.thedrum.com/news/2022/06/14/world-s-best-ads-ever-4-old-spice-ignites-comeback-with-the-man-your-man-could-smell.

Chapter 10

1. Infosys.com. https://www.infosys.com/age-of-ai.html.
2. Business Insider. https://www.businessinsider.com/vital-named-to-board-2014-5.

3. Nikkei Asia. https://asia.nikkei.com/Business/Artificial-intelligence-gets-a-seat-in-the-boardroom.
4. CNN. https://www.cnn.com/2014/09/30/business/computers-ceo-boardroom-robot-boss/.
5. Moravec, Hans (1988), *Mind Children*, Harvard University Press.
6. Teramind. https://www.teramind.co/.
7. Veriato. https://www.veriato.com/products/veriato-cerebral-insider-threat-detection-software.
8. ActivTrak. https://www.activtrak.com/product/productivity-reports/.
9. ITPro.com. https://www.itpro.co.uk/business-strategy/careers-training/359370/microsoft-patents-tech-to-combat-employee-stress.
10. NYT. https://www.nytimes.com/interactive/2022/08/14/business/worker-productivity-tracking.html.
11. Risk Management. http://www.rmmagazine.com/articles/article/2020/11/02/-Big-Business-or-Big-Brother-The-Risks-of-Employee-Monitoring-.
12. Ibid.

Chapter 11

1. Branson, Richard (2013). *Like a Virgin*. Great Britain: Virgin Books. p. 62. ISBN 978-0753519929.
2. Harvard. https://www.health.harvard.edu/blog/learning-new-skill-can-slow-cognitive-aging-201604279502.
3. Pew Research. https://www.pewresearch.org/internet/2017/05/03/the-future-of-jobs-and-jobs-training/.
4. https://medium.com/xcelerator-alg/great-leaders-are-lifelong-learners-8c613eee9143.
5. CNBC. https://www.cnbc.com/2017/11/15/warren-buffett-and-mark-cuban-agree-reading-is-key-to-success.html.

LeaderLogic® Services

LeaderLogic provides management consulting and training services to both emerging startups and global organizations. We also provide a wide range of certification and certificate training. These consulting and training programs are completely customized for the unique and special needs of our clients. Contact us today to learn more about:

Consulting Services

- Leadership development strategies
- Leadership optimization and problem-solving
- Board of Directors facilitation, management, and problem-solving
- Management consulting services
- Customer experience strategies
- Employee happiness and cultural transformation
- Innovation management and leadership

- Enterprise growth and sales development
- Executive communications and executive brand building

For additional information on our consulting services, please visit www.goleaderlogic.com.

Training Services

- Leadership Development Training
- Leadership workshops, and coaching
- Certified Ethical Sales Professional® (CESP)
- Certified Impactful Communicator™ (CIC)
- Certified Master of Customer Experience™ (CMCX)
- Certified Customer Relationship Advocate™ (CCRA)
- Customer Champion® Certificate (CCC)
- Innovation Superstar® Training

Additional training programs include training for Patient Experience, Association Leadership Certification Training, and Healthcare Executive Certification Training. All of our programs are available in live or virtual formats.

For additional information about our training services please visit www.mylearnlogic.com.

Need a Keynote Speaker or Trainer for your upcoming event?

Our Speakers Bureau provides leading professional Keynote Speakers and Trainers for the best Association and Enterprise events in the world. Visit our Speakers Bureau at www.keynoteology.com.

Book Nicholas Webb or Chase Webb to speak at your event!

To book Nicholas or Chase for an upcoming event, visit www.nickwebb.com.

About the Authors

The father-and-son team of Nicholas and Chase Webb bring the fresh perspective of a multigenerational view of how employees and team members view leadership and work.

Nicholas is a multiple number one bestselling author and internationally known leadership speaker and consultant. His clients represent dozens of the top brands in the world, including McDonald's, Pfizer, 3M, Johnson & Johnson, FedEx, Salesforce, and others.

Chase is a business development executive and a past associate consultant, who despite his young age has worked in the trenches to see these principles work with amazing returns on the time and effort investment.

www.ingramcontent.com/pod-product-compliance
Lightning Source LLC
Chambersburg PA
CBHW021710210326
41599CB00013B/1603